Grilling

GENERAL EDITOR
CHUCK WILLIAMS

RECIPES
JOHN PHILLIP CARROLL

PHOTOGRAPHY
ALLAN ROSENBERG

TIME
LIFE
BOOKS

TIME-LIFE BOOKS

Time-Life Books is a division of Time Life Inc.
Time-Life is a trademark of Time Warner Inc. U.S.A.

Time-Life Custom Publishing
Vice President and Publisher: Terry Newell
Managing Editor: Donia Ann Steele
Director of Acquisitions: Jennifer L. Pearce
Vice President of Sales and Marketing: Neil Levin
Director of Financial Operations: J. Brian Birky

WILLIAMS-SONOMA
Founder and Vice Chairman: Chuck Williams
Book Buyer: Victoria Kalish

WELDON OWEN INC.
President: John Owen
Vice President and Publisher: Wendely Harvey
Chief Operating Officer: Larry Partington
Managing Editor: Laurie Wertz
Consulting Editor: Norman Kolpas
Copy Editor: Sharon Silva
Design/Editorial Assistant: Janique Poncelet
Design: John Bull, The Book Design Company
Production: Stephanie Sherman, James Obata,
    Mick Bagnato
Production Coordinator: Tarji Mickelson
Vice President International Sales: Stuart Laurence
Co-Editions Director: Derek Barton
Food Photographer: Allan Rosenberg
Additional Food Photography: Allen V. Lott
Primary Food & Prop Stylist: Sandra Griswold
Food Stylist: Heidi Gintner
Prop Assistant: Karen Nicks
Glossary Illustrations: Alice Harth

The Williams-Sonoma Kitchen Library
conceived and produced by Weldon Owen Inc.
814 Montgomery St., San Francisco, CA 94133

In collaboration with Williams-Sonoma
3250 Van Ness Ave., San Francisco, CA 94109

Printed in China by Toppan Printing Co., LTD.

A Note on Weights and Measures:
All recipes include customary U.S. and metric
measurements. Metric conversions are based on
a standard developed for these books and have
been rounded off. Actual weights may vary.

A Weldon Owen Production

Copyright © 1992 Weldon Owen Inc.
Reprinted in 1992; 1992; 1993; 1993; 1993; 1994; 1994;
    1994; 1994; 1994; 1995; 1995; 1995; 1995; 1995; 1995;
    1996; 1996; 1996; 1997; 1997; 1998
All rights reserved, including the right of
reproduction in whole or in part in any form.

Library of Congress
Cataloging-in-Publication Data:

Carroll, John Phillip.
    Grilling / general editor, Chuck Williams ;
recipes, John Phillip Carroll ; photographs,
Allan Rosenberg.
        p.   cm.   — (The Williams-Sonoma kitchen library)
    Includes index.
    ISBN 0-7835-0206-0
—ISBN 0-7835-0207-9
    1. Barbecue cookery   I. Williams, Chuck.   II.   Title.
III. Series.
TX840.B3C34   1992
641.5'784—dc20   92-10316
                                            CIP

Contents

CHICKEN & POULTRY 17

BEEF, LAMB & PORK 45

FISH & SHELLFISH 75

VEGETABLES 89

INTRODUCTION

Grilling offers the home cook more latitude for creativity than any other way of preparing food. No wonder, then, that it is fast becoming the most popular cooking method of all.

That widespread appeal, I believe, stems from grilling's utter simplicity—with open flames or glowing coals or embers supplying the heat, and food cooking quickly on a metal grid. You, the cook, are more completely in charge of the process than an oven or stove top allows you to be. You build and control the fire. You raise or lower the grill and turn the food as it cooks. You select the seasonings—marinades, basting sauces, or such finishing touches as compound butters—to complement flavors that result from smoke and searing.

This volume celebrates the immediacy of grilling in all its variety. It begins with the basic, up-to-date information you need to start grilling, from facts about barbecues and other equipment to tips on fuels and fire starting, marinating and cooking techniques, and sauces and other flourishes. This overview is followed by 44 recipes that exemplify the varied nature of grilling, organized into chapters by featured ingredient—poultry, beef, lamb, pork, seafood and vegetables—with each recipe designed to spark your own creative variations.

Let me hasten to add that almost all of these recipes will cook as well on a small, inexpensive hibachi—or in some instances a stove-top grill or even under a broiler—as they will on a big outdoor barbecue. A more elaborate piece of equipment will simply make it easier to cook larger items or greater quantities, and may offer more subtle control over the heat and the cooking process.

No matter what equipment you have now, please don't hesitate to start trying these recipes, and join millions of other cooks in experiencing the thrill of the grill.

Chuck Williams

FIRE-BUILDING BASICS

Sorting through the many options available in grills, fuels and aromatics

No method of cooking could be more basic than building a fire and putting food over the glowing coals. But modern manufacturers provide the grill cook with options to suit every taste and budget. Grills themselves range from simple to sophisticated, making anything possible from quick cooking to long, slow roasting and smoking.

Charcoal is the fuel of choice. Mound it with paraffin-saturated starter blocks or pile it into a chimney starter (see page 10), then light with kitchen matches. The coals are ready for cooking when covered in light gray ash or when they glow red at night, about 30 minutes.

For direct-heat cooking, which is appropriate for relatively quick-cooking items such as hamburgers, steaks and most seafood, spread out the hot coals and place the food on the grill rack 4–6 inches (10–15 cm) directly above them. For items that take longer to cook, use the indirect-heat method: Spread the coals along the perimeter of the fire pan and place the food near the center of the grill rack, so that it cooks more slowly by radiant heat.

Aromatics—vine trimmings, woody basil stems, wood chips, dried or fresh herbs—flavor food with their fragrant smoke. Soak in water before using, then toss onto the hot coals during cooking. With gas grills, place aromatics on heavy-duty aluminum foil.

Hibachi
Relatively small, metal or cast-iron Japanese-style grill, usually square or rectangular in shape. Hibachis are especially convenient for balcony or patio use; adequately sized to cook for two or three people.

1. Paraffin-Saturated Corn Cobs
Buried in charcoal or wood and lighted for easy, nontoxic fire-starting that is free of fumes.

2. Kitchen Matches
Select long, sturdy, moisture-proof wooden kitchen matches that will strike on any surface.

3. Vine Cuttings
Soaked and spread over hot coals to add fruity flavor.

4. Charcoal Briquettes
Compact, uniform fuel compressed from pulverized charcoal and an additive that facilitates lighting and burning. Provides steady, spark-free heat. Avoid self-igniting briquettes, which may violate air-quality control standards. Store in a dry place.

5. Hardwood Charcoal
Lumps of hardwood—mesquite, hickory, alder, oak, apple, pecan, cherry—that have been burned just until charred. Break large chunks into smaller, more uniform pieces before lighting the fire. The charcoal will throw off sparks at first (watch carefully). Store in a dry place.

6. Dried Basil Stems
Soaked and spread over hot coals to add basil flavor.

7. Mesquite Chips
8. Hickory Chips
9. Apple Wood Chips
10. Alder Chips
Soaked and spread over hot coals to add subtle, smoky flavor.

11. Smoking Herbs
Dried herbs—sold individually or mixed, loose or in bags—to be soaked, squeezed free of excess moisture, and added to coals.

Electric Countertop Grill
Stick-resistant metal grill surfaces are electrically heated to three preset temperatures—300°F, 390°F or 480°F (150°C, 200°C or 250°C)—for easy indoor grilling. Entire hinged unit may be opened flat for a larger cooking surface.

Smoker-Grill
Adaptable, covered apparatus that efficiently stacks a domed cover, wire grill, water pan and fire pan, making it suitable for outdoor smoking, roasting, steaming or grilling.

Gas Grill
An alternative to charcoal-fueled grills. Gas burners heat enameled grids or lava rocks that not only give off the same kind of heat as glowing coals, but also vaporize drippings to produce smoke and channel off excess grease to prevent flare-ups. High grill hood allows roasting as well as grilling.

Electric Smoker
Smokes and cooks food on its wire shelves by indirect heat from fragrant wood smoldering in an electrically heated box, reproducing the effects of a traditional pit barbecue.

Kettle Grill
A deep fire pan and a domed cover, both vented for temperature control, permit long, slow, indirect-heat cooking of larger items as well as faster direct-heat grilling. Available in a range of sizes from small to large, kettle grills are more fuel-efficient and versatile than the common, shallow-pan, brazier-type backyard grill.

EQUIPMENT

All the tools you might need, from the spark that lights the fire to the final scrubbing of the grill

The array of grilling equipment at the cook's disposal may well dazzle those who love gadgets—and dismay those who yearn for simplicity.

But in fact, the many items shown here fulfill just a few basic functions. The tools you select will largely depend upon the kinds of food you like to grill and what works best for you.

In the end, one good tool that you use repeatedly is worth a score of clever items that don't really suit the way you cook.

1. Grill Cleaning Brushes
Long-handled brush has rustproof bristles and a stainless-steel scraper. Coil-shaped wire scraper attacks stubborn spots.

2. Spatulas
Choose sturdy spatulas with long wooden handles and durable stainless-steel blades. All-purpose spatula (far left) includes serrated cutting edge, teeth for scraping grill, and a bottle opener. Basic spatula (left center) is good for everyday grilling. Fish spatula (right center) has a concave, horizontal blade. Spatula with long rectangular blade (right) is perfect for steaks and hamburgers.

3. Stick-Resistant Spatula
Lighter-weight spatulas with stick-resistant blades are ideal for turning delicate items.

4. Spray Bottle
Sends stream or spray of water to control coals, promote steam or smoke, or moisten food.

5. Oil Can
For drizzling food with oil to prevent sticking.

6. Skewers
For holding small pieces of food on the grill rack. Available in stainless steel, wood or bamboo. Before using, soak wood and bamboo skewers in water for 30 minutes to prevent burning.

7. Salt and Pepper Shakers
Sturdy, oversized, stainless-steel shakers allow easy seasoning.

8. Flashlights
For outdoor grilling after dark.

9. Tapered Tongs
Scissor-action tongs with stick-resistant tapered ends for handling rounded foods such as corn or shellfish.

10. Double Skewers
Parallel pairs of stainless-steel skewers anchor large, oddly shaped items.

11. Forks
Choose sturdy forks for placing and turning foods such as steaks or poultry pieces.

12. Small Tongs
Allows mess free turning of small items while marinating.

13. Instant-Read Thermometer
Inserts into meat or poultry to measure doneness in seconds.

14. Grill Thermometer
Attaches magnetically to grill rack to give surface temperature.

15. Basting Brushes
Choose sturdy brushes with well-attached natural bristles.

16. Stainless-Steel Tongs
Spring-hinged restaurant-style tongs for a variety of tasks.

17. Spark Lighter
Electronically generates a spark for easy lighting of fires.

EQUIPMENT: ACCESSORIES

Optional equipment—from mitts and gloves to special grill racks—that make work easier for the outdoor cook

None of the equipment shown here is absolutely essential for successful grilling. But each item, in its own way, makes the task go more smoothly and with less possibility of mishap.

A chimney fire starter, for example, offers one of the simplest, most ecologically sound ways to get coals glowing brightly. Sturdy mitts and gloves provide cooks with a firm grip and ample protection from tools and grills heated by a well-made fire.

An array of special grill racks has been developed to hold large, small or delicate foods—steaks, whole fish or small pieces of seafood—that might otherwise stick to the grill or be difficult to turn. These rest directly on top of the standard metal cooking grid that comes with your grill.

And inclement weather or a lack of outdoor space needn't stop the determined griller. Thanks to devices like the simple stove-top grill shown here, as well as electric countertop grills (see pages 6–7), basic grilling can be easily accomplished indoors.

WILLIAMS-SONOMA

1

2

3

4

5

6

7

8

9

1. Apron
Heavy-duty denim stands up to outdoor use. Pockets hold small tools.

2. Standard Grill Rack
Circular brazier type is shown, although shape will vary with model. Chrome-plating makes for easier cleaning.

3. Chimney Fire Starter
Charcoal is loaded into the top; crumpled newspaper is loosely stuffed under the baffle in the bottom. Once the paper is ignited, the coals are ready for cooking in about 20 minutes. Pour them into the fire pan using the heat-resistant handle.

4. Griffo™ Grill
For grilling seafood or vegetables, with small holes that allow heat to come through while preventing food from falling into the fire.

5. Hinged Fish Grill
Two-sided, wire-hinged, elongated construction encloses whole fish or fillets.

6. Hinged Grill
Two-sided and hinged to enclose large steaks or fish fillets securely. Long handle aids in turning and includes latch to hold food in place. Smaller sizes are available for hamburgers.

7. Stove-Top Grill
Stick-resistant, domed surface is grooved and vented to drain off fat into a water-filled drip pan for mess-free grilling on a cooktop.

8. Oven Mitt and Pot Holders
Made of heavy quilted denim for good protection from heat, with one side treated for fire resistance.

9. Leather Barbecue Glove
Provides maximum protection from heat when cooking over large grills or intense fires. Gauntlet extension shields the cook's forearm from the heat.

MARINATING FOR FLAVOR AND TEXTURE

Perhaps the easiest way to express your creativity in grilling is to marinate food before you cook it. Steeping meat, poultry, seafood or vegetables for anywhere from a few minutes to several hours in a mixture usually consisting of some sort of acidic liquid (citrus fruit juice, wine or vinegar), oil, herbs and spices imparts flavors that complement the natural taste of the foods. What's more, a marinade adds moisture to foods, particularly if it is also used for basting.

One claim made about marinating—that it tenderizes food—is highly overrated. While acid does break down protein fibers to some small degree, only long, slow cooking can truly make a tough cut of meat tender.

The photographs on the right demonstrate three simple techniques for marinating. Most people simply place the food in a nonreactive (ceramic or glass) container just large enough to hold it. Heavy-duty plastic bags are also convenient: Since they keep the food completely surrounded by the marinade, they eliminate the need for frequent turning.

Dry marinades—blends of herbs or spices without added liquid—are sometimes used to season fish and other delicately flavored foods.

Choose a nonreactive (glass or ceramic) dish just large enough to hold the food and marinade. Turn the food every 30 minutes or so.

Put the food and marinade together in a heavy-duty, self-sealing plastic bag, carefully forcing out any air when sealing.

To flavor food with a dry mixture of seasonings, lightly coat with oil and then pat generously on all sides with the mixture.

Red or White Wine Marinade

This recipe can be made with red wine for beef and lamb or white wine for poultry. Large roasts and whole chickens can marinate anywhere from 1–3 days; the longer they marinate, the more flavor they will gain.

1 bottle, about 3½ cups (28 fl oz/875 ml), dry
    red or white wine
½ cup (4 fl oz/125 ml) olive oil
1 onion, finely chopped
4 tablespoons chopped fresh parsley
2 large cloves garlic, minced
1 tablespoon chopped fresh thyme, rosemary or
    tarragon, or 2 teaspoons dried herb of choice
1 teaspoon salt
½ teaspoon freshly ground pepper

In a large bowl whisk together all the ingredients. Use immediately or refrigerate in a tightly covered jar for up to 2 days.

*Makes about 5 cups
(40 fl oz/1.25 l),
enough for large
roast, leg of
lamb or whole
chicken*

Citrus Marinade

Citrus juice gives a clean, satisfying flavor to chicken, veal or fish. Use an herb that is compatible with the food you are marinating, such as thyme or tarragon for veal, sage for pork, dill or tarragon for fish. Let steaks, chops and fish fillets marinate for at least an hour, or all day if you wish. Large cuts can marinate for a day or two.

½ cup (4 fl oz/125 ml) olive oil
¼ cup (2 fl oz/60 ml) fresh lemon juice
1 clove garlic, minced
2 tablespoons finely chopped shallots or green (spring)
    onions
2 teaspoons grated lemon zest
2 teaspoons chopped fresh thyme, tarragon, dill or
    sage, or 1 teaspoon dried herb of choice
½ teaspoon salt
½ teaspoon freshly ground pepper

In a small bowl whisk together all the ingredients. Use immediately or refrigerate in a tightly covered jar for up to 2 days.

*Makes about 1 cup (8 fl oz/250 ml), enough for 2–3 lb
(1–1.5 kg) veal or pork chops, steaks or fish fillets*

Citrus Marinade

White Wine Marinade

Dry Marinades

Dry mixtures of salt, pepper, herbs and spices rubbed over food several hours before grilling are good flavor enhancers. Rub the meat, poultry or fish lightly with oil before coating it with the marinade. Made with fresh herbs, these marinades will keep if refrigerated, tightly covered, up to 3 days. Made with dried herbs, they will keep, stored airtight in a cupboard, for several weeks.

FOR LAMB, BEEF AND CHICKEN:
2 tablespoons chopped fresh rosemary or
    2 teaspoons dried rosemary
2 large cloves garlic, minced
1½ teaspoons salt
1 teaspoon freshly ground pepper
finely grated zest of 1 lemon or lime

FOR FISH:
2 tablespoons chopped fresh dill or 2 teaspoons
    dried dill
2 teaspoons mild paprika
1 tablespoon grated lemon zest
1 teaspoon salt
1 teaspoon freshly ground pepper
¼ teaspoon cayenne pepper

FOR PORK:
2 tablespoons chopped fresh thyme or
    2 teaspoons dried thyme
1 tablespoon chopped fresh sage or
    1 teaspoon dried sage
2 teaspoons salt
1 teaspoon freshly ground pepper
¼ teaspoon ground allspice or cloves
2 cloves garlic, minced

*S*elect the list of ingredients that complements the food you are marinating. In a small bowl stir together the ingredients.

Each recipe makes about 4 tablespoons if made with fresh herbs, enough for 4–5 lb (2–2.5 kg) beef, pork or lamb, or 2 lb (1 kg) fish

Basic Barbecue Sauce

A traditional American barbecue sauce, good on chicken, spareribs and hamburgers. Because the sauce contains sugar it burns easily, and should be brushed on for the last 10–15 minutes of cooking. Pass any remaining sauce at the table.

2 tablespoons vegetable oil
1 onion, finely chopped
3 cloves garlic, minced
1½ cups (16 oz/500 g) catsup (tomato sauce)
½ cup (4 fl oz/125 ml) cider vinegar
¼ cup (2 fl oz/60 ml) Worcestershire sauce
⅓ cup (3 oz/90 g) sugar
1 tablespoon chili powder
½ teaspoon, more or less, cayenne pepper

*H*eat the oil in a saucepan over moderate heat and add the onion and garlic. Cook gently, stirring, for about 5 minutes. Add the catsup, vinegar, Worcestershire sauce, sugar, chili powder and cayenne to taste (the more cayenne you use, the hotter it will be). Reduce the heat and simmer, partially covered, until the sauce has thickened slightly, about 20 minutes.

Makes about 2½ cups (20 fl oz/625 ml)

Red Wine Barbecue Sauce

Lighter than the preceding sauce, and good to brush on chicken, pork, beef and lamb every 20 minutes or so.

1 cup (8 fl oz/250 ml) dry red wine
⅓ cup (3 fl oz/80 ml) red wine vinegar
¼ cup (2 fl oz/60 ml) olive oil
3 tablespoons Worcestershire sauce
1 onion, finely chopped
1 tablespoon sugar
1 tablespoon grated orange zest
2 cloves garlic, minced

*I*n a saucepan combine the wine, vinegar, oil, Worcestershire sauce, onion, sugar and orange zest. Bring to a boil, then reduce the heat and simmer, partially covered, for 25 minutes. This sauce remains quite thin. Remove from the heat and stir in the garlic.

Makes about 2 cups (16 fl oz/500 ml)

Basic Barbecue Sauce

Above: Red Wine Barbecue Sauce

Compound Butters

A slice of flavored butter placed on a hot-from-the-grill steak, hamburger, chop, fish fillet or piece of chicken melts to form an almost-instant bit of sauce. Compound butters keep for several days in the refrigerator or may be frozen for several months. The herb butter is especially good on steaks, chops and hamburgers, while the lemon butter enhances fish and chicken. Pork and beef are good with the mustard butter.

FOR HERB BUTTER:

½ cup (4 oz/125 g) unsalted butter, at room temperature

2 tablespoons chopped fresh tarragon, sage or cilantro (coriander/Chinese parsley) or 2 teaspoons dried tarragon or sage

2 tablespoons chopped fresh parsley

½ teaspoon salt

½ teaspoon freshly ground pepper

FOR LEMON BUTTER:

½ cup (4 oz/125 g) unsalted butter, at room temperature

4 tablespoons chopped fresh parsley

2 tablespoons fresh lemon juice

2 teaspoons finely grated lemon zest

½ teaspoon salt

¼ teaspoon freshly ground pepper

FOR MUSTARD BUTTER:

½ cup (4 oz/125 g) unsalted butter, at room temperature

3 tablespoons Dijon mustard

2 tablespoons chopped shallots or green (spring) onions

1 tablespoon chopped fresh parsley

1–2 teaspoons fresh lemon juice

½ teaspoon salt

¼ teaspoon freshly ground pepper

Select the compound butter that complements the food you are serving. In a bowl beat the butter with a wooden spoon or hand-held mixer until smooth, then gradually beat in all the remaining ingredients. Form the butter mixture into a rough log about 4 inches (10 cm) long and 1 inch (2.5 cm) in diameter. Wrap in plastic wrap and chill until firm. To serve, cut into slices ½ inch (12 mm) thick.

Serves 6–8

Herbed Butterflied Squab

1½ teaspoons salt
1 teaspoon freshly ground pepper
2 tablespoons chopped fresh thyme or
  2 teaspoons dried thyme
1 teaspoon crushed bay leaf
2 teaspoons crushed juniper berries
4 squabs (young pigeons), about 1 lb
  (500 g) each, butterflied
olive oil
handful of fresh thyme sprigs, optional

Small birds such as squabs and quail grill quickly and are good for a festive dinner—if you're not timid about eating with your fingers! Your butcher can butterfly them for you. Squab has dark, richly flavored meat, and a dry rub of salt, pepper and herbs gives a nice background of flavor. Serve with sautéed potatoes and mustard greens or spinach, and follow with a watercress-and-tomato salad.

In a small bowl stir together the salt, pepper, thyme, bay leaf and juniper berries. Rub each squab lightly with olive oil, then sprinkle each bird with one fourth of the herb mixture and rub it gently into the skin. Place the birds on a large platter or in an enameled baking pan, laying them flat, and cover with plastic wrap. Marinate in the refrigerator for at least 2 hours, or overnight is even better.

If using the thyme sprigs, soak in water to cover for about 30 minutes. Prepare a fire in a grill. Position the oiled grill rack 4–6 inches (10–15 cm) above the fire. Arrange the squabs, breast side down, on the rack. Grill for 15–20 minutes, turning them two or three times and brushing once or twice with oil. Squab is done when the skin is well browned and the meat is slightly pink when slashed to the bone in the thickest part. The last few minutes of cooking, place a sprig of damp thyme under each bird. The sprigs will smoke gently, giving off a pleasant aroma and flavor.

Serves 4

Lemon-Rosemary Chicken

½ cup (4 fl oz/125 ml) fresh lemon
   juice
⅓ cup (3 fl oz/80 ml) olive oil
2 tablespoons chopped shallots
2 tablespoons chopped fresh rosemary
½ teaspoon salt
½ teaspoon freshly ground pepper
1 frying chicken, about 3½ lb
   (1.75 kg), quartered
handful of fresh rosemary sprigs

Fresh rosemary gives chicken an irresistible flavor, and a few sprigs tossed on the fire during the last few minutes of cooking impart a pleasant smokiness. Rosemary, by the way, is very easy to grow in your garden.

Combine the lemon juice, oil, shallots, rosemary, salt and pepper and mix well. Place the chicken quarters in a large plastic food storage bag and pour in the marinade. Press the air out of the bag and seal it tightly. Massage the bag gently to distribute the marinade. Set the bag in a large bowl and refrigerate for at least 2 hours, or all day if more convenient, turning and massaging the bag occasionally.

Soak the rosemary sprigs in water to cover for about 30 minutes. Prepare a fire in a grill. Position the oiled grill rack 4–6 inches (10–15 cm) above the fire.

Remove the chicken quarters from the marinade and pat them dry with absorbent paper towels; reserve the marinade. Arrange the chicken quarters, skin side down, on the rack. Grill, turning frequently, for 30–35 minutes. The last 10 minutes, drop the soaked rosemary sprigs on the fire and brush the chicken two or three times with the reserved marinade. If the chicken starts to get too dark, turn skin side up and move it to a cooler part of the rack, so it isn't directly over the fire, or cool the fire a little by covering the grill and opening the vents halfway.

Serves 2–4

Lemon Chicken Breasts

½ cup (4 fl oz/125 ml) fresh lemon
 juice
½ cup (4 fl oz/125 ml) fresh orange
 juice
2 cloves garlic, minced
1 tablespoon grated fresh ginger
1 tablespoon chopped fresh tarragon or
 1 teaspoon dried tarragon
½ teaspoon salt
¼ teaspoon freshly ground pepper
6 chicken breast halves, skinned and
 boned

Skinless, boneless chicken breast halves cook quickly and are low in calories. If you wish to enrich them a bit, top each breast with a pat of lemon butter (recipe on page 15) just before serving.

In a small bowl stir together the lemon juice, orange juice, garlic, ginger, tarragon, salt and pepper. Arrange the chicken breasts in a shallow glass or porcelain dish or enameled baking pan and pour the lemon juice mixture evenly over them. Marinate in the refrigerator, turning occasionally, for 2–3 hours.

   Prepare a fire in a grill. Position the oiled grill rack 4–6 inches (10–15 cm) above the fire. Remove the chicken from the marinade and pat it dry with absorbent paper towels; reserve the marinade. Arrange the chicken on the rack. Grill, turning two or three times and brushing with the reserved marinade, until the chicken is no longer pink in the center, 15–20 minutes.

Serves 6

Teriyaki Chicken

⅓ cup (3 fl oz/80 ml) soy sauce
⅓ cup (3 fl oz/80 ml) dry sherry
¼ cup (2 fl oz/60 ml) vegetable oil
2 tablespoons sugar
2 cloves garlic, minced
1 tablespoon grated fresh ginger
1 frying chicken, about 3½ lb
   (1.75 kg), cut into serving pieces

A Polynesian classic, teriyaki was originally brought to the mainland by travelers from Hawaii. The soy-and-ginger marinade, also a favorite for flank steak and lamb kabobs, penetrates the meat with its complex flavors. Serve with the mixed vegetable grill on page 94, if you wish, and rice.

In a small bowl stir together the soy sauce, sherry, oil, sugar, garlic and ginger. Place the chicken in a large plastic food storage bag and pour in the soy mixture. Press out the air and seal the bag tightly. Massage the bag gently to distribute the marinade. Set the bag in a large bowl and refrigerate for at least 2 hours, or all day if you wish, turning and massaging the bag occasionally.

Prepare a fire in a grill. Position the oiled grill rack 4–6 inches (10–15 cm) above the fire.

Remove the chicken pieces from the marinade and pat them dry with absorbent paper towels; reserve the marinade. Arrange the chicken pieces on the rack, skin side down. Grill, turning frequently, 30–35 minutes. During the last 10 minutes of cooking, brush the chicken two or three times with the reserved marinade. If the chicken starts to get too dark, turn it skin side up and move it to a cooler part of the grill, so it is not directly over the fire, or cool the fire a little by covering the grill and opening the vents halfway.

Serves 2–4

Thyme and Mustard Quail

⅓ cup (4 oz/125 g) Dijon mustard
½ cup (4 fl oz/125 ml) dry white or
   red wine
⅓ cup (3 fl oz/80 ml) olive oil
1 tablespoon chopped fresh thyme or
   1 teaspoon dried thyme
8 quail, about 5 oz (155 g) each
salt
freshly ground pepper

Cooks who never hesitate to barbecue chicken and turkey are often apprehensive about grilling quail because they are less common. Do not be shy about these single-serving birds. Their succulent, dark meat is moist and delicious. Just take care not to overcook them.

*Prepare a fire in a grill. Position the oiled grill rack 4–6 inches (10–15 cm) above the fire.

In a small bowl stir together the mustard, wine, 3 tablespoons of the oil and the thyme; set aside. Pat the quail dry with absorbent paper towels. Rub them with the remaining olive oil and sprinkle lightly with salt and pepper.

Place the quail, breast side down, on the rack. Grill for about 8 minutes, turning them frequently to brown evenly. Brush the mustard mixture on the quail and cook for about 5 minutes longer, turning them once and brushing again with the mustard mixture. Do not overcook the birds; the meat should remain slightly pink at the bone.

Serves 4

Grill-Roasted Turkey

1 turkey, 10–12 lb (5–6 kg)

2 tablespoons olive oil

2 tablespoons chopped fresh rosemary
   or 2 teaspoons dried rosemary

salt

freshly ground black pepper

2 lemons, quartered

large handful of fresh sage, tarragon or
   parsley sprigs

½ cup (4 oz/125 g) unsalted butter,
   melted

2 tablespoons fresh lemon juice

This comes out juicy, with a smoky flavor and dark brown skin. A roasting chicken may be done the same way: For a 5–6 lb (2.5–3 kg) bird, halve all the ingredients and cook for about 90 minutes total, or to the suggested temperature on a meat thermometer.

Soak 3 handfuls (about 5 oz/155 g) hickory chips in water to cover for about 1 hour. Prepare a fire for indirect-heat cooking in a covered grill (see page 6). Position the oiled grill rack 4–6 inches (10–15 cm) above the fire.

Pat the turkey dry with absorbent paper towels and rub with the olive oil and rosemary. Sprinkle inside and out with salt and pepper. Tuck the lemon quarters and herb sprigs inside the cavity; truss the bird. Drop half of the wood chips on the fire. Place the turkey, breast side up, in the center of the rack. Cover the grill and cook for 1 hour.

In a small bowl stir together the butter and lemon juice. Drop the remaining wood chips on the fire. Brush the turkey with half of the butter mixture, then cover and cook for 45 minutes longer, adding more coals if necessary to maintain a constant temperature. Brush with the remaining butter mixture, then cook covered for 30–45 minutes longer, or until a meat thermometer registers 170°F (80°C) in the breast or 185°F (85°C) in the thigh. Total cooking time is about 2½ hours. Remove the turkey and let it rest for 15–20 minutes before carving.

Serves 10–12

Chicken Liver Brochettes

8 slices bacon (about 8 oz/250 g), cut
  into 2-inch (5-cm) lengths
¼ cup (2 fl oz/60 ml) olive oil
1 tablespoon soy sauce
½ cup (1½ oz/45 g) chopped green
  (spring) onions, including white and
  green portions, plus 6 extra, white
  portion only, cut into 2-inch (5-cm)
  lengths
2 teaspoons chopped fresh thyme or
  oregano, or ½ teaspoon dried thyme
  or oregano
½ teaspoon freshly ground pepper
2 lb (1 kg) chicken livers, trimmed and
  halved

*Chicken livers should be removed from the grill when still
slightly pink inside; overcooking toughens them and ruins
their smooth texture. Other poultry livers, such as duck,
turkey and goose, may be cooked in the same way. Grilled
onion slices (recipe on page 98) would complement these
brochettes nicely.*

*B*ring a saucepan filled with water to a boil, add the bacon
pieces and blanch for 3 minutes. Drain well and pat dry
with absorbent paper towels. Set aside.

In a large bowl combine the oil, soy sauce, chopped green
onions, thyme or oregano and pepper. Stir well, then add
the chicken livers and toss to coat. The livers may be grilled
now, or you may cover the bowl and marinate them in the
refrigerator, tossing occasionally, for 1 or 2 hours.

Prepare a fire in a grill. Position the oiled grill rack 4–6
inches (10–15 cm) above the fire. Thread the liver, bacon
and green onion pieces alternately onto 6 skewers. Reserve
any of the marinade remaining in the bowl. Arrange the
skewers on the rack. Grill, turning occasionally and
brushing once or twice with the reserved marinade, until
the livers are well browned outside and slightly pink inside,
8–12 minutes.

Serves 6

All-American Barbecued Chicken

5–6 lb (2.5–3 kg) chicken pieces
salt
freshly ground pepper
basic barbecue sauce (recipe on page 14)

If your barbecued chicken tends to flare up on the grill and get too dark, the following method of direct- and indirect-heat cooking will give you perfect results. "Frying" chickens, birds weighing 3–4 lb (1.75–2 kg) each, are good for grilling. If you like assorted pieces, use the whole chicken, cut up. Or buy any other chicken parts you like, such as thighs, breasts or legs. Brush the sauce on for just the last few minutes of cooking so it doesn't burn. Serve with corn grilled in the husk (recipe on page 101) and potato salad or coleslaw.

P repare a fire for indirect-heat cooking in a covered grill (see page 6 for detailed instructions). Position the oiled grill rack 4–6 inches (10–15 cm) above the fire.

Sprinkle the chicken pieces on both sides with salt and pepper. Place them, skin side down, around the edge of the grill rack so they are directly above the hot coals. Grill, uncovered, turning frequently, until well browned, 10–15 minutes. Watch the chicken constantly, and have a spray bottle of water handy to douse flare-ups. Move the chicken pieces to the middle of the grilling rack—they may overlap slightly—so that they are no longer directly over the fire.

Cover the grill and open the vents halfway. Cook for 10 minutes. Turn the chicken, brush it with the sauce, re-cover and cook for 5 minutes more. Brush again with the sauce, then cover and cook until the chicken is no longer pink when cut at the bone, about 5 minutes longer. Pass the remaining sauce at the table.

Serves 4–6

Cornish Game Hens with Ginger Butter

2 shallots or green (spring) onions, finely chopped

3 large cloves garlic, chopped

¼ cup (2 oz/60 g) unsalted butter, at room temperature

2 tablespoons grated fresh ginger

2 tablespoons chopped fresh parsley

½ teaspoon salt, plus extra for sprinkling

¼ teaspoon freshly ground pepper, plus extra for sprinkling

4 Cornish game hens, about 1½ lb (750 g) each

Game hens are inclined to be dry, but a garlic-ginger butter rubbed under the skin tempers that tendency, and makes these birds juicy and flavorful.

Prepare a fire in a covered grill. Position the oiled grill rack 4–6 inches (10–15 cm) above the fire.

In a bowl combine the shallots or green onions, garlic, butter, ginger, parsley, ½ teaspoon salt and ¼ teaspoon pepper. Beat with a wooden spoon until blended.

Starting at the neck end of each bird, gently slide your fingers under the skin covering the breast, gradually working them between the flesh and skin down toward the thighs. Proceed slowly so you do not tear the skin.

Divide the butter mixture into 4 fairly equal-sized portions and slip a portion under the skin of each bird. With your fingertips work the ginger butter under the skin, covering all of the breast meat and easing it toward the thighs as best you can. Sprinkle each body cavity with salt and pepper. Truss each bird.

Place the hens, breast side up, on the rack. Grill for about 20 minutes. Turn them breast down and cover the grill, opening the vents halfway. Cook until the meat is no longer pink when cut at the bone, 20–25 minutes longer.

Serves 4

Buffalo Wings

FOR THE MARINADE:
1 cup (8 fl oz/250 ml) cider vinegar
2 tablespoons vegetable oil
2 tablespoons Worcestershire sauce
2 tablespoons chili powder
1 teaspoon red pepper flakes
1 teaspoon salt
1 teaspoon freshly ground pepper
1 tablespoon Tabasco (hot red pepper)
  sauce

4 lb (2 kg) chicken wings (about 24)

FOR THE BLUE CHEESE SAUCE:
⅔ cup (5 fl oz/160 ml) sour cream
½ cup (4 fl oz/125 ml) mayonnaise
1 large clove garlic, minced
2 teaspoons Worcestershire sauce
1 cup (4 oz/125 g) crumbled blue cheese
salt
freshly ground pepper
2 tablespoons, more or less, milk

celery sticks

These spicy chicken wings, served with celery sticks and blue cheese sauce for dipping, gained popularity at the Anchor Bar in Buffalo, New York. They are good hot or cold, and make perfect finger food to take to a backyard potluck or a picnic. Make them spicier or milder as you please by altering the amounts of chili powder and Tabasco sauce.

To make the marinade, in a small bowl stir together the vinegar, oil, Worcestershire sauce, chili powder, red pepper flakes, salt, pepper and Tabasco sauce. Place the chicken wings in a large plastic food storage bag and pour in the marinade. Press out the air and seal the bag tightly. Massage the bag gently, to distribute the marinade. Set in a large bowl and refrigerate for several hours, turning and massaging the bag occasionally.

To make the blue cheese sauce, in a small bowl whisk together the sour cream, mayonnaise, garlic, Worcestershire sauce and blue cheese. Season to taste with salt and pepper. Add enough milk to make a sauce with the consistency of pancake batter. Cover and refrigerate.

Prepare a fire in a grill. Position the oiled grill rack 4–6 inches (10–15 cm) above the fire. Remove the wings from the marinade and pat them dry with absorbent paper towels; reserve the marinade. Arrange the wings on the rack. Grill, turning frequently and brushing with the reserved marinade, until cooked through, 25–30 minutes. Serve with the dipping sauce and celery sticks.

Serves 4 as a main course, 6–8 as an appetizer

Chicken and Mushroom Kabobs

1¼ teaspoons salt

1 teaspoon freshly ground pepper

1 teaspoon dried sage

½ teaspoon dried thyme

½ teaspoon cayenne pepper

1 clove garlic, minced

4 chicken breast halves, skinned and boned

1 tablespoon vegetable oil

12 large fresh cultivated (button) mushrooms, stemmed

12–16 fresh sage leaves, optional

2 tablespoons olive oil

A dry marinade of herbs and salt brings out the natural flavor of chicken and forms a crisp, spicy coating.

In a small bowl stir together 1 teaspoon of the salt, the pepper, sage, thyme, cayenne pepper and garlic; set aside.

Cut the chicken breasts into strips about 3 inches (7.5 cm) long and 1 inch (2.5 cm) wide. Pat them dry with absorbent paper towels and place in a large bowl. Add the vegetable oil and toss to coat the chicken strips evenly. Add the herb mixture and toss again to coat completely. Let stand for about 1 hour.

Prepare a fire in a grill. Position the oiled grill rack 4–6 inches (10–15 cm) above the fire.

Toss the mushroom caps with the sage leaves (if desired) and olive oil and the remaining ¼ teaspoon salt. Thread the chicken strips onto skewers alternately with the mushroom caps and sage leaves. Arrange the skewers on the rack. Grill, turning frequently, until the chicken and mushrooms are lightly browned and the chicken is cooked through, 8–10 minutes.

Serves 4

Mustard-Grilled Chicken

⅔ cup (6 oz/180 g) Dijon mustard
2 tablespoons cayenne pepper
¼ cup (2 fl oz/60 ml) vegetable oil
2 tablespoons wine vinegar
1 broiler chicken, about 2½ lb
  (1.25 kg), split

Mustard is wonderful with chicken, and in this recipe it does double duty as both a marinade and a basting sauce. The mixture is very spicy; if you desire less hot seasoning, reduce the amount of cayenne to 2 teaspoons.

❧

Stir together ⅓ cup (3 oz/90 g) of the mustard, 1 tablespoon of the cayenne pepper, the vegetable oil and vinegar. Place the chicken in a large plastic food storage bag and pour in the mustard mixture. Press out the air and seal tightly. Massage gently to distribute the marinade. Set in a large bowl and refrigerate for at least 2 hours, or all day if you wish, turning and rubbing the bag occasionally.

Prepare a fire for indirect-heat cooking in a covered grill (see page 6 for detailed instructions). Position the oiled grill rack 4–6 inches (10–15 cm) above the fire.

Combine the remaining ⅓ cup (3 oz/90 g) mustard with the remaining 1 tablespoon cayenne pepper. Remove the chicken from the marinade, allowing as much marinade as possible to cling to the surface.

Place the chicken, skin side down, on the rack. Grill, turning frequently, for about 25 minutes; do not worry if some of the marinade sticks to the grill. Have a spray bottle of water handy to douse flare-ups. Turn the chicken skin side up and brush it with the mustard-cayenne mixture. Cover the grill, open the vents halfway and cook until no longer pink when cut at the bone, about 10 minutes longer.

Serves 2–4

Hickory-Smoked Chicken

1 roasting chicken, 5–6 lb (2.5–3 kg)
½ lemon
salt
freshly ground pepper
sprigs of fresh rosemary or parsley
several slices of fresh ginger
1 tablespoon vegetable oil or olive oil

Dropping aromatic hickory chips on the fire gives this chicken a smoky taste. It is good served hot or cold. Accompany it with mayonnaise flavored with a bit of mustard, a rice or pasta salad and crusty bread.

Soak 3 handfuls (about 5 oz/155 g) hickory chips in water to cover for about 1 hour.

Prepare a fire for indirect-heat cooking in a covered grill (see page 6 for detailed instructions). Position the oiled grill rack 4–6 inches (10–15 cm) above the fire.

Pat the chicken dry with absorbent paper towels. Rub the outside of the chicken with the cut side of the lemon. Sprinkle the bird inside and out with salt and pepper to taste. Tuck sprigs of parsley or rosemary and the ginger inside the cavity. Rub the skin with the oil; truss the bird.

Drop half of the soaked wood chips on the fire. Place the chicken, breast side down, on the rack and cover the grill. After about 40 minutes, carefully turn the bird breast side up and sprinkle the remaining wood chips on the fire. Cook until the chicken is no longer pink when cut at the bone, about 1 hour, adding more coals to the fire if necessary to maintain a constant temperature. The chicken is done when a meat thermometer registers 170°F (80°C) in the breast or 185°F (85°C) in the thigh. Remove the chicken from the grill and let it rest for about 10 minutes before carving.

Serves 4

Stuffed Turkey Breast

½ cup (4 oz/125 g) unsalted butter

½ cup (2½ oz/75 g) finely chopped celery

½ cup (2½ oz/75 g) finely chopped onion

3 cups (6 oz/185 g) fresh white bread crumbs

1 teaspoon dried thyme

1 teaspoon dried sage

⅓ cup (2 oz/60 g) raisins

⅓ cup (1½ oz/45 g) chopped walnuts

salt

freshly ground pepper

¼ cup (2 fl oz/60 ml) chicken stock or turkey stock, if needed

1 turkey breast, 6–8 lb (3–4 kg), boned and butterflied, with skin intact

vegetable oil

A boned and butterflied turkey breast cooks quickly and is easy to carve. Your butcher will butterfly it for you.

Melt the butter in a frying pan. Add the celery and onion and cook until they are soft, about 5 minutes. Transfer to a large bowl. Add the bread crumbs, thyme, sage, raisins and walnuts and mix well. Season to taste with salt and pepper. It should be moist but not wet. If too dry, add the stock.

Soak 3 handfuls (about 5 oz/155 g) hickory chips or oak chips in water to cover for about 1 hour. Place the turkey breast, skin side down, on a work surface; you will have two large flaps of meat. Sprinkle with salt and pepper. Spread the stuffing over one flap of meat and down the center of the breast, then fold the other flap over it. With heavy string (preferably linen; it does not char easily), tie the breast together in 4 or 5 places to make a tight, cylindrical roll. Rub with oil and sprinkle with salt and pepper.

Prepare a fire for indirect-heat cooking in a covered grill (see page 6). Position the oiled grill rack 4–6 inches (10–15 cm) above the fire. Drop half of the wood chips on the fire. Place the rolled breast in the center of the rack, cover the grill and open the vents halfway. Cook for about 1 hour, turning twice. Sprinkle the remaining chips on the fire and add more coals if necessary. Cook for 45 minutes–1 hour longer. It is done when a meat thermometer registers 170°F (80°C). Remove from the grill; cover loosely with foil for 10 minutes. Remove the strings, then cut into slices.

Serves 8–10

Tenderloin Pepper Steaks

4 beef tenderloin (fillet) steaks, 6–8 oz
 (185–250 g) each
salt
4 tablespoons coarsely crushed black
 peppercorns
½ recipe herb butter or mustard butter
 (recipes on page 15)

*If you like black pepper, you know how good this dish is.
Any tender steak, such as a T-bone or New York, may be
prepared the same way. To coarsely crush peppercorns,
smash them with the bottom of a heavy saucepan.*

❈

Sprinkle each steak lightly with salt, then rub about ½
tablespoon coarsely crushed peppercorns into each side,
pressing the pepper firmly into the meat.

 Prepare a fire in a grill. Position the oiled grill rack 4–6
inches (10–15 cm) above the fire. Arrange the steaks on
the rack. Grill, turning them every 1 or 2 minutes, about
8 minutes' total cooking time for rare or about 10 minutes'
total cooking time for medium. Top each steak with a slice
of the flavored butter before serving.

Serves 4

Gingered Skirt Steak

1 lime
½ cup (4 fl oz/125 ml) dry red wine
⅓ cup (3 fl oz/80 ml) soy sauce
2 tablespoons grated fresh ginger
2 cloves garlic, minced
1 tablespoon sugar
dash of Tabasco (hot red pepper) sauce
3 lb (1.5 kg) beef skirt steak

Skirt steak is the diaphragm muscle, and it has a rich, beefy flavor. Although it is relatively inexpensive, skirt steak is sometimes hard to find, so you might have to order it specially. Be sure to have the butcher skin it for you. Served with grilled onions on a crusty French roll, it makes a great steak sandwich.

Grate the zest from the lime then juice it. In a small bowl stir together the lime zest and juice, wine, soy sauce, ginger, garlic, sugar and Tabasco sauce. Place the meat in a glass or porcelain dish or enameled baking pan large enough for it to lie flat. Pour the marinade evenly over the steak and then turn the meat to coat both sides. Cover and refrigerate for at least 3 hours, or all day if you wish, turning the meat occasionally.

Prepare a fire in a grill. Position the oiled grill rack 4–6 inches (10–15 cm) above the fire. Remove the meat from the marinade; reserve the marinade. Pat the meat dry with paper towels and place it on the rack. Grill for 6–8 minutes, turning every minute or so and brushing two or three times with the reserved marinade. Skirt steak is best served rare, and will toughen if overcooked. Cut into serving pieces.

Serves 6

Peppery Flank Steak

2 tablespoons fresh lime juice
grated zest of 1 lime
2 cloves garlic, minced
½ teaspoon hot chili oil
¼ cup (2 fl oz/60 ml) vegetable oil
1 teaspoon red pepper flakes
½ cup (4 fl oz/125 ml) dry red wine
1 tablespoon sugar
2 tablespoons soy sauce
1½ lb (750 g) flank steak

Because a flank steak is a thin piece of meat, the flavor of a marinade penetrates it completely. Serve this peppery beef rare, with grilled green onions and tomatoes, and skewered or baked potatoes.

✻

*I*n a small bowl stir together the lime juice, lime zest, garlic, chili oil, vegetable oil, red pepper flakes, wine, sugar and soy sauce. Place the meat in a shallow glass or porcelain dish or enameled baking pan. Pour the mixture over the steak, cover with plastic wrap and marinate in the refrigerator for at least 2 hours—all day is better—turning the meat occasionally and basting with the marinade.

Prepare a fire in a grill. Position the oiled grill rack 4–6 inches (10–15 cm) above the fire. Remove the steak from the marinade and pat it dry with absorbent paper towels; reserve the marinade. Place the steak on the rack. Grill for 10–12 minutes, turning once and brushing two or three times with the reserved marinade; the meat should be on the rare side.

To serve, carve on the diagonal into thin slices.

Serves 4

Marinated Beef Tenderloin with Tarragon Butter

red wine marinade (*recipe on page 12*)
1 beef tenderloin (fillet), about 4 lb
　(2 kg) after trimming
½ cup (4 oz/125 g) unsalted butter, at
　room temperature
2 tablespoons chopped fresh tarragon or
　2 teaspoons dried tarragon
2 tablespoons chopped fresh parsley
1 tablespoon fresh lemon juice
½ teaspoon salt
½ teaspoon freshly ground pepper

Tenderloin is costly, but it's the most succulent cut of beef, with no bone and no waste. Have the butcher trim it for you, and plan ahead so you can marinate it for at least a day.

✹

Prepare the marinade. Place the beef in a plastic food storage bag and pour in the marinade. Press out the air and seal the bag tightly. Massage the bag gently to distribute the marinade. Set in a large bowl and refrigerate for several hours, or all day if you prefer, turning and massaging the bag occasionally.

Meanwhile, in a bowl combine the butter, tarragon, parsley, lemon juice, salt and pepper and beat by hand with a wooden spoon. Shape into a rough log about 4 inches (10 cm) long and 1 inch (2.5 cm) wide, wrap in plastic wrap and chill until firm.

Prepare a fire in a covered grill. Position the oiled grill rack 4–6 inches (10–15 cm) above the fire. Remove the meat from the marinade and pat it dry with absorbent paper towels. Place the meat on the rack. Grill, turning it frequently to brown all sides, for about 20 minutes. Cover the grill, open the vents halfway and cook until a meat thermometer registers 130°F (55°C) for rare or 140°F (60°C) for medium. Remove from the grill, place on a warm platter, cover loosely with foil and let rest for 10 minutes.

Carve the tenderloin into slices ¾–1 inch (2–2.5 cm) thick. Top each serving with a pat of tarragon butter.

Serves 6–8

51

Spicy Barbecued Brisket

1 beef brisket, 4–5 lb (2–2.5 kg),
    trimmed of excess fat
3 cloves garlic, cut into slivers
2 tablespoons vegetable oil
1 tablespoon coarse or kosher salt
1½ teaspoons dried thyme
1 teaspoon freshly ground pepper
1 teaspoon paprika
1 teaspoon cayenne pepper
basic barbecue sauce *(recipe on page 14)*

Like many less-tender cuts of beef, inexpensive brisket is a real bargain in taste, with an intense beef flavor that is enhanced by spicy marinades and sauces. Cook it slowly and carve it into thin slices. Have plenty of barbecue sauce and crusty bread to pass at the table.

❋

Make several slits in the surface of the brisket and poke a sliver of garlic into each one. Rub the brisket with the oil. In a small bowl stir together the salt, thyme, pepper, paprika and cayenne pepper and rub over the meat.

Prepare a fire for indirect-heat cooking in a covered grill (see page 6 for detailed instructions). Position the oiled grill rack 4–6 inches (10–15 cm) above the fire. Place the brisket on the rack so it is not directly over the coals, cover the grill and cook for 1 hour, turning once. Brush with some of the sauce and cook 1–1¼ hours longer, turning and brushing lightly with sauce two or three times more. Remove from the grill and let rest for 10 minutes.

Carve into thin slices across the grain. Arrange on a warmed platter and spoon a little sauce over the top. Pass the remaining sauce in a bowl at the table.

Serves 8–10

Herbed Rack of Lamb

1 rack of lamb, about 2 lb (1 kg), with
  8 ribs
1 clove garlic, cut into slivers
vegetable oil or olive oil
2 tablespoons dry marinade for lamb
  (recipe on page 13)

*Depending upon the rest of your menu—and the appetites of
your guests—one rack of lamb will serve two or three people.
Round out the meal with such dishes as grilled eggplant,
potatoes and polenta.*

❋

Prepare a fire in a grill. Position the oiled grill rack 4–6
inches (10–15 cm) above the fire.

Trim off the outside fat from the rack of lamb; do not
worry about removing every single bit. For a special-
occasion dinner, you may want to trim the meat from the
last 2 or 3 inches (5 or 7.5 cm) of each rib bone, then scrape
the bones clean with a knife.

Make a small slit between each rib and insert a sliver of
garlic. Rub the meat lightly with oil, then rub it with the dry
marinade. If you have scraped the bones, cover the exposed
tips with a strip of foil so that they do not burn.

Place the lamb on the rack. Grill, turning several times,
about 25 minutes, or until a meat thermometer registers
140°F (60°C). Cut the ribs apart into individual chops
to serve.

Serves 2 or 3

Lamb and Potato Skewers

12 small boiling potatoes

2 lb (1 kg) lean, boneless lamb, cut into
   1½-inch (4-cm) cubes

½ cup (4 fl oz/125 ml) olive oil

1 tablespoon chopped fresh rosemary

1 tablespoon fresh lemon juice

¼ teaspoon salt

¼ teaspoon freshly ground pepper

Meat and potatoes can share the same skewer as long as they will cook in about the same amount of time. Cubes of tender beef may also be skewered this way. If you have them, sturdy branches of fresh rosemary, about 8 inches (20 cm) long and soaked in water to cover for about 2 hours, make aromatic and unusual skewers.

❋

Prepare a fire in a grill. Position the oiled grill rack 4–6 inches (10–15 cm) above the fire.

Cook the potatoes in boiling salted water to cover until they are barely tender when pierced, about 10 minutes. Drain well and cover with cold water. Let stand for about 2 minutes, then drain again and pat dry with absorbent paper towels. Thread the potatoes alternately with the lamb onto skewers.

In a small bowl whisk together the oil, rosemary, lemon juice, salt and pepper. Arrange the skewers on the rack. Grill for 6–8 minutes, turning two or three times and brushing with the olive oil mixture. Take care not to over-cook the lamb; it should remain pink in the center.

Serves 4–6

Butterflied Leg of Lamb

FOR THE MINT SAUCE:
½ cup (4 fl oz/125 ml) cider vinegar
⅓ cup (3 oz/90 g) sugar
⅔ cup (1 oz/30 g) chopped fresh mint
  leaves
pinch of salt

FOR THE LAMB:
⅔ cup (5 fl oz/160 ml) dry red wine
⅓ cup (3 fl oz/80 ml) olive oil
2 tablespoons chopped shallots
1 tablespoon chopped fresh rosemary or
  1 teaspoon dried rosemary
2 cloves garlic, minced
½ teaspoon salt
½ teaspoon freshly ground pepper
1 leg of lamb, 6–7 lb (3–3.5 kg), boned,
  butterflied and trimmed of visible fat

A butterflied leg of lamb is a large, flat, boneless piece of meat weighing about 4 lb (2 kg); your butcher can prepare it for you. This goes best with the basics: garlicky mashed potatoes, potatoes grilled or roasted with rosemary, or rice pilaf. The tart mint sauce suggested here bears no resemblance to the sweet mint jelly often served with lamb.

✻

*T*o make the mint sauce, combine the vinegar and sugar in a small saucepan and bring to a boil, stirring just until the sugar dissolves. Remove from the heat and add the mint and salt; set aside to allow the flavors to mellow.

To prepare the lamb, place it in a glass or porcelain dish or enameled baking pan large enough for it to lie flat. Stir together the wine, oil, shallots, rosemary, garlic, salt and pepper. Pour over the lamb and marinate for at least 2 hours, or all day if you wish, turning occasionally.

Prepare a fire in a grill. Position the oiled grill rack 4–6 inches (10–15 cm) above the fire. Remove the lamb from the marinade and pat it dry with absorbent paper towels; reserve the marinade. Place the lamb on the rack. Grill for 35–45 minutes, turning frequently and brushing occasionally with the reserved marinade. The meat should remain pink inside; make a small cut in the thickest part to check.

Remove from the grill and let rest for 5 minutes, covered loosely with aluminum foil. Carve across the grain into thin slices. Serve with the mint sauce.

Serves 6

Rosemary-Smoked Lamb Chops

6–8 sprigs of fresh rosemary
¼ cup (2 fl oz/60 ml) olive oil
2 tablespoons chopped fresh rosemary
½ teaspoon salt
¼ teaspoon freshly ground pepper
8 rib or loin lamb chops, about 1 inch
   (2.5 cm) thick, trimmed of visible fat

Loin or rib lamb chops about 1 inch (2.5 cm) thick are the best type for grilling because they brown well outside and remain pink in the center. These are as good at room temperature as they are hot from the grill.

✺

*P*repare a fire in a grill. Position the oiled grill rack 4–6 inches (10–15 cm) above the fire.

Soak the rosemary sprigs in water to cover for about 30 minutes before beginning to grill.

In a small bowl whisk together the oil, chopped rosemary, salt and pepper. Rub a small amount of this mixture over the surface of each chop. Reserve the remainder to brush on the chops as they cook.

Drop a few damp rosemary sprigs on the fire. Arrange the chops on the rack. Grill, turning two or three times and brushing lightly with the remaining rosemary mixture, until browned but still pink in the center, about 8 minutes. Drop the remaining rosemary sprigs on the fire midway through the cooking.

Serves 4

Saffron Lamb Kabobs

½ teaspoon saffron threads

½ cup (4 fl oz/125 ml) beef stock,
  boiling

½ cup (4 fl oz/125 ml) dry red or
  white wine

2 tablespoons vegetable oil

½ teaspoon ground cardamom

½ teaspoon salt

¼ teaspoon freshly ground pepper

2 lb (1 kg) lean, boneless lamb, cut into
  1½-inch (4-cm) cubes

Tender cubes of lamb cut from the leg work well for kabobs. Serve on a bed of rice pilaf. Although saffron is expensive, its special flavor is worth the cost. You will extract more essence from a small amount if you first steep it in hot water or stock.

☀

*I*n a large bowl stir together the saffron and beef stock and let stand for at least 30 minutes. Add the wine, oil, cardamom, salt and pepper. Add the lamb cubes and toss to combine. Cover and refrigerate for at least 3 hours, tossing occasionally.

Prepare a fire in a grill. Position the oiled grill rack 4–6 inches (10–15 cm) above the fire. Remove the lamb from the marinade, reserving the marinade. Pat the meat dry with absorbent paper towels, then thread it onto skewers. Arrange the skewers on the rack. Grill, turning frequently and brushing occasionally with the reserved marinade, until browned but still pink in the center, about 8 minutes.

Serves 4–6

All-American Barbecued Spareribs

6 lb (3 kg), more or less, pork spareribs,
   in 2 slabs
salt
freshly ground pepper
basic barbecue sauce (*recipe on page 14*)

Sticky, spicy and delicious. Serve coleslaw and potato salad with this time-honored favorite, and have plenty of paper napkins on hand.

☀

Prepare a fire for indirect-heat cooking in a covered grill (see page 6 for detailed instructions). Position the oiled grill rack 4–6 inches (10–15 cm) above the fire.

Sprinkle the ribs generously on both sides with salt and pepper. Place them on the rack so they are not directly over the fire, cover the grill and open the vents halfway. Cook for 45 minutes, turning once.

Brush the tops of the ribs with some of the sauce, cover the grill and cook for 10 minutes longer. Turn the ribs, brush with a little more sauce, then cover and cook for a final 10–15 minutes.

Cut the slabs into single-rib pieces and mound on a warmed platter. Pass the remaining sauce at the table.

Serves 4–6

Curried Pork Saté

¼ cup (2 fl oz/60 ml) soy sauce

¼ cup (2 fl oz/60 ml) vegetable oil

¼ cup (2 fl oz/60 ml) dry red or white wine

1 tablespoon sugar

2 teaspoons curry powder

½–1 teaspoon red pepper flakes

2½ lb (1.25 kg) lean, boneless pork, cut into 1½-inch (4-cm) cubes

Satés are strips or pieces of meat that are soaked in a spicy marinade—the more red pepper flakes you use, the spicier they will be. Like all skewered meats, they cook quickly and are easy to do even on a small grill. Serve on a bed of rice, along with chutney or a tart fruit relish. Tender lamb may be prepared in the same way, although it will need to cook for only 8–10 minutes.

※

In a bowl stir together the soy sauce, oil, wine, sugar, curry powder and pepper flakes. Add the pork and toss to coat well. Cover and refrigerate for at least 2 hours, tossing occasionally.

Prepare a fire in a grill. Position the oiled grill rack 4–6 inches (10–15 cm) above the fire.

Remove the pork from the marinade and pat dry with absorbent paper towels; reserve the marinade. Thread the pork onto skewers. Arrange the skewers on the rack. Grill, turning frequently and brushing occasionally with the reserved marinade, until cooked through, about 20 minutes.

Serves 6

Orange-and-Ginger-Glazed Pork Roast

2 tablespoons vegetable oil, if needed
1 boneless pork loin, 3½–4 lb (1.75–2 kg), tied for roasting
dry marinade for pork (*recipe on page 13*), optional
½ cup (5 oz/155 g) orange marmalade
⅓ cup (3 oz/90 g) Dijon mustard
1 tablespoon grated fresh ginger
1 tablespoon Worcestershire sauce
¼–½ teaspoon salt
¼–½ teaspoon freshly ground pepper

The optional dry marinade helps bring out the natural flavor of pork, and the orange-ginger mixture gives the meat a dark, spicy glaze. Since boneless pork loin is so easy to carve and serve, this is a good recipe to double for a crowd. Accompany it with grilled apple rings or applesauce.

☀

*I*f you are using the marinade, rub the oil over the pork, then coat it evenly with the dry marinade. Let stand for at least 1 hour, or cover and refrigerate for several hours.

Meanwhile, in a small bowl stir together the marmalade, mustard, ginger, Worcestershire sauce, salt and pepper.

Prepare a fire for indirect-heat cooking in a covered grill (see page 6 for detailed instructions). Position the oiled grill rack 4–6 inches (10–15 cm) above the fire.

Place the pork on the rack so it is not directly over the fire, cover the grill and open the vents halfway. Cook for 45 minutes, then turn the roast. Add more coals if necessary to maintain a constant temperature. Cook for 40–50 minutes longer, brushing with the marmalade mixture every 10 minutes and turning once or twice. The pork is done when a meat thermometer registers 160°F (70°C).

Remove from the grill, cover loosely with aluminum foil and let rest for 10 minutes. To serve, snip the strings and cut into slices ¼ inch (6 mm) thick.

Serves 8

Mustard-Glazed Spareribs

2 tablespoons vegetable oil
1 small onion, chopped
1 cup (12 oz/375 g) honey
1 cup (8 oz/250 g) Dijon mustard
½ cup (4 fl oz/125 ml) cider vinegar
½ teaspoon salt, plus salt to taste
1 teaspoon ground cloves
6 lb (3 kg), more or less, baby back ribs,
   in slabs
freshly ground pepper

The amount of mustard-honey basting sauce is generous, because you'll want plenty to pass at the table. For a smoky flavor, toss a couple handfuls of damp hickory chips onto the fire. You may, if you wish, substitute 2 slabs of regular spareribs for the baby back ribs.

❋

*H*eat the vegetable oil in a saucepan over moderate heat. Add the onion and cook until soft, about 5 minutes. Add the honey, mustard, vinegar, ½ teaspoon salt and the cloves. Stir well and bring to a boil. Reduce the heat and simmer for about 5 minutes, stirring occasionally. Remove from the heat and set aside.

Prepare a fire for indirect-heat cooking in a covered grill (see page 6 for detailed instructions). Position the oiled grill rack 4–6 inches (10–15 cm) above the fire. Generously salt and pepper the ribs on both sides. Place the ribs on the rack, cover the grill and open the vents halfway. Cook for 40 minutes, turning once. Add more coals to the fire if necessary to maintain a constant temperature.

Brush the tops of the ribs with some of the honey mixture, then cover and cook 10 minutes longer. Turn the ribs, brush with a little more sauce, cover and cook for 10 minutes. Total cooking time is approximately 1 hour. Remove from the grill and cut into single-rib pieces. Mound on a warmed platter and pass any remaining sauce at the table.

Serves 4–6

Pork Tenderloins with Guacamole

½ cup (4 fl oz/125 ml) dry red or
  white wine

2 tablespoons balsamic vinegar or red
  or white wine vinegar

2 tablespoons olive oil or vegetable oil

2 teaspoons chopped fresh thyme or
  ½ teaspoon dried thyme

½ teaspoon salt, plus extra for
  sprinkling

¼ teaspoon freshly ground pepper,
  plus extra for sprinkling

2 lb (1 kg), more or less, pork tenderloins (fillets), trimmed of visible fat

2 or 3 large ripe avocados

1 large ripe tomato, peeled, seeded and
  chopped

1 clove garlic, minced

2 tablespoons chopped fresh cilantro
  (coriander/Chinese parsley)

2 tablespoons or more fresh lime juice

¼ teaspoon, more or less, Tabasco
  (hot red pepper) sauce

1 teaspoon minced fresh jalapeño
  (hot green) chili pepper, optional

warm tortillas

Pork today is quite lean, which means it can sometimes be dry. Tenderloins seem to be reliably tender and juicy if they are not overcooked.

✳

Stir together the wine, vinegar, oil, thyme, the ½ teaspoon salt and the ¼ teaspoon ground pepper. Place the tenderloins in a glass or porcelain dish or enameled baking pan just large enough to hold them comfortably in one layer. Pour the wine mixture evenly over the pork. Cover and refrigerate for at least 2 hours, turning occasionally.

Peel and pit the avocados and place them in a bowl. Mash them coarsely with a fork, leaving a few small lumps. Add the tomato, garlic and cilantro, then mix in the lime juice, Tabasco sauce, jalapeño, if desired, and salt and pepper to taste. Press a piece of plastic wrap directly onto the surface of the guacamole and refrigerate until serving.

Prepare a fire in a grill. Position the oiled grill rack 4–6 inches (10–15 cm) above the fire. Remove the tenderloins from the marinade and pat them dry with absorbent paper towels; reserve the marinade. Place the tenderloins on the rack. Grill for about 25 minutes, brushing the meat occasionally with the reserved marinade and turning it frequently so it browns evenly. It is done when a meat thermometer registers 160°F (70°C). Remove from the grill and let rest for 5 minutes before carving. Cut on the diagonal into thin slices. Serve with the guacamole and tortillas.

Serves 4–6

Fennel-Marinated Salmon

2 large fennel bulbs, with tops intact

½ cup (4 fl oz/125 ml) olive oil

3 tablespoons fresh lemon juice

½ teaspoon salt

¼ teaspoon freshly ground pepper

4 salmon steaks or skinless fillets,
6–8 oz (185–250 g) each and about
1 inch (2.5 cm) thick

½ recipe lemon butter (recipe on page
15), optional

If you can't locate fennel, use chopped fresh dill or cilantro in place of the fennel tops and serve the fish with grilled Belgian endive (first blanched for a minute) or sautéed cucumbers.

Chop enough of the feathery fennel tops to measure about 4 tablespoons. In a small bowl whisk together the chopped fennel, ¼ cup (2 fl oz/60 ml) of the oil, the lemon juice, salt and pepper. Arrange the fish in a single layer in a shallow glass or porcelain dish or enameled baking pan. Pour the fennel mixture evenly over the fish and turn the fish to coat both sides. Cover and refrigerate for 30 minutes–1 hour, turning once.

Trim off and discard the remaining fennel tops and cut each bulb in half lengthwise. Cook the fennel bulbs in boiling salted water until just tender when pierced, 7–10 minutes. Drain well; set aside.

Prepare a fire in a grill. Position the oiled grill rack 4–6 inches (10–15 cm) above the fire. Remove the fish from the marinade; reserve the marinade. Arrange the fish and fennel bulbs on the rack. Grill for about 10 minutes; the fish is done when it has turned from translucent to opaque throughout. During cooking turn the fish once or twice, brushing it lightly with the reserved marinade; turn the fennel four or five times, brushing it lightly with the remaining ¼ cup (2 fl oz/60 ml) oil.

Remove the fish and fennel to a warmed platter and, if you wish, top each piece of fish with a pat of lemon butter.

Serves 4

Snapper with Cilantro Butter

FOR THE CILANTRO BUTTER:

¼ cup (2 oz/60 g) unsalted butter, at room temperature

3 tablespoons chopped fresh cilantro (coriander/Chinese parsley)

1½ tablespoons fresh lemon or lime juice

1 teaspoon grated lemon or lime zest

¼ teaspoon salt

pinch of freshly ground pepper

FOR THE FISH:

2 lb (1 kg) skinless red snapper fillets, cut into 4 equal pieces each about 1 inch (2.5 cm) thick

vegetable oil

salt

freshly ground pepper

True red snapper comes from the Gulf of Mexico and the Atlantic coast of the Americas from the Carolinas south to Brazil. It has a firm texture and a mild flavor. Salmon or bass may also be prepared this way.

To make the cilantro butter, combine the butter, cilantro, lemon or lime juice and zest, salt and pepper in a bowl and beat by hand with a wooden spoon. Shape into a rough log about 2 inches (5 cm) long and 1 inch (2.5 cm) in diameter, wrap in plastic wrap and chill until firm.

Prepare a fire in a grill. Position the oiled grill rack 4–6 inches (10–15 cm) above the fire. Rub the fish lightly with oil and sprinkle to taste with salt and pepper. Arrange the fish on the rack. Grill, turning once, about 10 minutes; the fish is done when it turns from translucent to opaque throughout.

Remove to a warmed platter or plates. Cut the cilantro butter into 4 equal slices and top each fillet with a slice.

Serves 4

Grilled Swordfish with Tomatillo Salsa

FOR THE SALSA:

6 fresh tomatillos

1 small red onion, cut into chunks

2 cloves garlic, cut into pieces

1 large fresh Anaheim chili pepper or other mild green chili pepper, halved, seeded and cut into pieces

½ fresh red or green jalapeño (hot) chili pepper, seeded and cut into pieces

4 tablespoons fresh cilantro (coriander/ Chinese parsley) sprigs

salt

FOR THE FISH:

4 swordfish steaks, 6–8 oz (185–250 g) each and about 1 inch (2.5 cm) thick

2 tablespoons vegetable oil

salt

freshly ground pepper

Because of its firm, meaty texture and oily flesh, swordfish is perfect for grilling, and a zesty fresh tomatillo salsa provides a nice contrast. Fresh tuna and shark are also good prepared this way. Tomatillos are a type of ground cherry native to Mexico. They can be found in Latin American shops and well-stocked supermarkets. Two or three ripe red tomatoes may be substituted. Serve this dish with warm tortillas.

❧

To make the salsa, remove and discard the papery husks from the tomatillos. Chop the tomatillos coarsely. In the work bowl of a food processor, combine the tomatillos, onion, garlic, Anaheim and jalapeño chilies and cilantro. Process just until coarsely chopped and transfer to a bowl. Or chop all of the ingredients coarsely by hand and combine them in a bowl. Season with salt to taste; set aside.

Prepare a fire in a grill. Position the oiled grill rack 4–6 inches (10–15 cm) above the fire. Rub the fish steaks with the oil and sprinkle them to taste with salt and pepper. Arrange the steaks on the rack. Grill, turning once or twice, for about 10 minutes; the fish is done when it has turned from translucent to opaque throughout.

Remove to a warmed platter. Place a spoonful of salsa on each steak. Pass the remaining salsa in a bowl at the table.

Serves 4

Scallop and Mushroom Brochettes

2 lb (1 kg) sea scallops

1 lb (500 g) large fresh cultivated (button) mushrooms

¼ cup (2 fl oz/60 ml) olive oil

2 tablespoons fresh lemon juice

2 tablespoons chopped fresh tarragon or 1 teaspoon dried tarragon

1 clove garlic, minced

½ teaspoon salt

¼ teaspoon freshly ground pepper

2 limes, cut into slices ¼ inch (6 mm) thick

Scallops grill quickly, so take care not to overcook them or they will be tough. Firm, meaty fish such as halibut, snapper and sea bass may be cut into 1½-inch (4-cm) chunks, skewered and grilled in this same way.

Remove and discard the small, flat muscle, or "foot," usually attached to the side of each scallop. Remove and discard the stems from the mushrooms.

In a large bowl whisk together the oil, lemon juice, tarragon, garlic, salt and pepper. Add the scallops and mushrooms and toss to coat evenly. Cover and refrigerate for 30 minutes, tossing once or twice.

Prepare a fire in a grill. Position the oiled grill rack 4–6 inches (10–15 cm) above the fire. Remove the scallops and mushrooms from the marinade; reserve the marinade. Alternate the scallops and mushrooms with the lime slices on 4 or 6 skewers. Arrange the skewers on the rack. Grill, turning frequently and brushing two or three times with the reserved marinade, until the scallops are just cooked through, 6–8 minutes.

Serves 4–6

Garlic-Skewered Shrimp

12–16 large whole cloves garlic, plus 3
  large cloves garlic, minced
2 lb (1 kg) large or jumbo shrimp
  (prawns)
⅓ cup (3 fl oz/80 ml) olive oil
¼ cup (2 fl oz/60 ml) tomato sauce
  (puréed tomatoes)
2 tablespoons red wine vinegar
2 tablespoons chopped fresh basil or
  1½ teaspoons dried basil
½ teaspoon salt
½ teaspoon cayenne pepper

*Like scallops, large shrimp grill quickly. Be careful not to
overcook them.*

$\backsim$

Drop the whole garlic cloves into a saucepan of rapidly
boiling water and blanch for 3 minutes. Drain well and
set aside.

Peel and devein the shrimp. In a large bowl stir together
the oil, tomato sauce, vinegar, basil, minced garlic, salt and
cayenne pepper. Add the shrimp and toss to coat evenly.
Cover and refrigerate for about 30 minutes, tossing once
or twice.

Prepare a fire in a grill. Position the oiled grill rack 4–6
inches (10–15 cm) above the fire. Remove the shrimp from
the marinade. There will be a little bit of marinade
remaining in the bowl; reserve it. Thread the shrimp and
garlic cloves alternately onto the skewers as follows: Bend
each shrimp almost in half, so that the large end nearly
touches the smaller tail end. Insert the skewer just above the
tail, so that it passes through the body twice. Follow each
shrimp or two with a garlic clove.

Arrange the skewers on the rack. Grill, turning them
frequently and brushing two or three times with the
reserved marinade, until the shrimp become pink, 6–8
minutes.

Serves 4–6

Halibut with Red Pepper Butter

FOR THE RED PEPPER BUTTER:
¼ cup (2 oz/60 g) unsalted butter, at
   room temperature
3 tablespoons chopped, roasted and
   peeled red sweet pepper
1 teaspoon chili powder
¼ teaspoon red pepper flakes
¼ teaspoon salt

FOR THE FISH:
4 halibut steaks, 6–8 oz (185–250 g)
   each and about 1 inch (2.5 cm) thick
vegetable oil
salt
freshly ground pepper

Halibut has a delicate taste that is perked up by a lively pepper butter. Peeled red sweet peppers, available in jars, have simplified the preparation of anything calling for peppers "roasted and peeled." Serve with grilled polenta (recipe on page 90).

To make the red pepper butter, combine the butter, roasted pepper, chili powder, pepper flakes and salt in a bowl and beat by hand with a wooden spoon. Shape into a rough log 2 inches (5 cm) long and 1 inch (2.5 cm) in diameter, wrap in plastic wrap and chill until firm.

Prepare a fire in a grill. Position the oiled grill rack 4–6 inches (10–15 cm) above the fire. Rub the fish lightly with oil and sprinkle to taste with salt and pepper. Arrange the fish on the rack. Grill, turning once, for about 10 minutes; the fish is done when it has turned from translucent to opaque throughout.

Transfer the fish to a warmed platter or plates. Cut the pepper butter into 4 equal slices and top each fish steak with a slice.

Serves 4

Salmon Skewers

2 lb (1 kg) skinless salmon fillets
½ cup (4 fl oz/125 ml) olive oil
2 tablespoons chopped fresh dill or
   2 teaspoons dried dill
2 tablespooons Pernod or other anise-
   flavored liqueur or brandy
½ teaspoon salt
½ teaspoon freshly ground pepper
2 lemons, sliced
sprigs of fresh parsley or dill
lemon wedges

Salmon stays moist and cooks quickly, so there's ample time to grill some vegetables or fruits over the same fire. The best cut to use for these skewers is a skinned and filleted salmon tail, which has few if any bones. Serve with herbed two-potato skewers (recipe on page 97) and fresh peas or grilled asparagus.

Cut the salmon into strips about 1 inch (2.5 cm) wide and 3 inches (7.5 cm) long. In a large bowl stir together the oil, dill, liqueur, salt and pepper. Add the salmon strips and toss to combine. Cover and refrigerate for about 30 minutes, tossing once or twice.

Prepare a fire in a grill. Position the oiled grill rack 4–6 inches (10–15 cm) above the fire. Remove the salmon from the marinade; reserve the marinade. Alternating them with the lemon slices, thread the salmon strips onto skewers, weaving each strip so that the skewer passes through it two or three times. Arrange the skewers on the rack. Grill, turning frequently and brushing with the reserved marinade, until the salmon is cooked through, 8–10 minutes.

Remove to a warmed platter and garnish with parsley or dill and lemon wedges.

Serves 4

Pepper and Summer Squash Skewers

1½ lb (750 g) zucchini (courgettes) or crookneck squashes or small pattypan squashes

1 green and 1 red bell pepper (capsicum)

⅓ cup (3 fl oz/80 ml) olive oil

2 tablespoons wine vinegar

1 clove garlic, minced

2 teaspoons chopped fresh thyme or ½ teaspoon dried thyme

½ teaspoon salt

¼ teaspoon freshly ground pepper

10–12 large fresh cultivated (button) mushrooms, stemmed

Use a combination of yellow and green squashes, if you can, and keep in mind that tiny pattypan squashes, about 1 inch (2.5 cm) or so in diameter, can be skewered and grilled whole. Serve these colorful skewers with saffron lamb kabobs (recipe on page 62) on a large platter of rice.

If the squash are large, cut them crosswise into pieces 1 inch (2.5 cm) long. Halve the bell peppers and remove the stems, ribs and seeds. Cut the peppers into 1-inch (2.5-cm) squares. Drop the zucchini and peppers into a large pot of boiling salted water and boil for 2 minutes. Drain well and cover with cold water. Let stand for 2 minutes, then drain again and pat dry with absorbent paper towels.

In a large bowl whisk together the oil, vinegar, garlic, thyme, salt and pepper. Add the blanched vegetables and the mushrooms and toss to combine. Let stand for about 30 minutes, tossing occasionally.

Prepare a fire in a grill. Position the oiled grill rack about 4 inches (10 cm) above the fire. Remove the vegetables from the marinade, reserving the marinade. Thread the pepper and squash pieces and mushrooms alternately onto skewers. Arrange the skewers on the rack. Grill, turning occasionally and brushing with the reserved marinade, until lightly browned, 8–10 minutes.

Serves 4

Grilled Polenta

3 cups (24 fl oz/750 ml) water

1 teaspoon salt

2 tablespoons unsalted butter

¾ cup (4 oz/125 g) polenta or yellow
   cornmeal

¾ cup (3 oz/90 g) freshly grated
   Parmesan cheese

¼ teaspoon cayenne pepper

olive oil

A slice of polenta is a good foundation for a grilled chicken breast or a butterflied squab or quail, and is an excellent accompaniment to steaks and chops. Few things are easier and better tasting.

Combine the water, salt and butter in a medium saucepan and bring to a boil. Gradually add the polenta or cornmeal, whisking constantly so it doesn't lump. Lower the heat and continue cooking, stirring frequently, until quite thick, 10–15 minutes. Remove from the heat and stir in the Parmesan cheese and cayenne.

Line a 9-inch (23-cm) pie plate with plastic wrap, letting it extend over the edges. Spread the polenta evenly over the plastic wrap and smooth the top with a spoon. Cover tightly with plastic wrap and chill until firm, at least 1 hour.

Prepare a fire in a grill. Position the oiled grill rack 4–6 inches (10–15 cm) above the fire. Invert the pie plate to unmold the polenta. Peel off the plastic wrap. Cut the polenta into 6 pie-shaped wedges. Brush each wedge lightly on both sides with oil. Arrange the polenta wedges on the rack. Grill, turning two or three times, until golden, about 10 minutes.

Serves 4–6

Grilled Tomatoes and Green Onions

⅓ cup (3 fl oz/80 ml) olive oil

1 tablespoon fresh lemon juice or wine vinegar

2 tablespoons chopped fresh basil

1 tablespoon chopped shallots

½ teaspoon salt

¼ teaspoon freshly ground pepper

3 large tomatoes, cut into slices ½–¾ inch (12 mm–2 cm) thick

10–12 green (spring) onions, trimmed, including 4 inches (10 cm) of green tops

sprigs of fresh basil or parsley

Firm tomatoes, even those that are slightly green, should be used for this recipe. They are less juicy and hold their shape better when grilled than fully ripe ones. Fresh basil is wonderful with tomatoes, but you could also use chopped tarragon or even parsley in the basting sauce. Serve warm or at room temperature, with grilled lamb or fish.

❧

*P*repare a fire in a grill. Position the oiled grill rack 4–6 inches (10–15 cm) above the fire.

In a small bowl stir together the oil, lemon juice or vinegar, chopped basil, shallots, salt and pepper.

Arrange the tomatoes and onions on the rack. Grill, turning them two or three times and brushing with the oil mixture, about 5 minutes. If the onions are large, they might take 1 or 2 minutes longer.

Transfer the tomatoes and onions to a platter and garnish with basil or parsley sprigs.

Serves 4–6

Mixed Vegetable Grill

¾ cup (6 fl oz/180 ml) olive oil

3 tablespoons fresh lemon juice

3 tablespoons chopped fresh cilantro
(coriander/Chinese parsley)

1 teaspoon salt

¼ teaspoon freshly ground pepper

2 fennel bulbs, trimmed and cut
in half lengthwise

4 baby artichokes, trimmed

2 whole heads garlic, unpeeled

2 Belgian endives (witloof/chicory)

2 Anaheim (mild green) chili peppers,
cut in half lengthwise, seeded and
deribbed

8 oz (250 g) whole fresh shiitake
mushrooms, stemmed

12–16 thin asparagus, about 12 oz
(375 g), trimmed

1 large red onion, cut crosswise into
slices ½ inch (12 mm) thick

Here is a suggested medley of vegetables, but improvise and use whatever is in season and reasonably young and tender. Very firm vegetables will grill more quickly and evenly if you first cook them in boiling water until just tender, a step that can be done hours ahead.

*In a small bowl whisk together the olive oil, lemon juice, cilantro, salt and pepper; set aside.

In a large pot bring about 4 qt (4 l) salted water to a rapid boil. Cook the fennel bulbs until just tender when pierced, 7–10 minutes. Remove them and drain well; set aside. Drop in the artichokes and cook until just tender, 5–10 minutes. Scoop them out, drain well and then cut them in half lengthwise; set aside. Blanch the garlic heads for about 5 minutes; remove them, drain well and set aside. Finally, blanch the Belgian endives for about 1 minute; remove them, drain well and then cut in half lengthwise. Set aside. Have the chili peppers, mushrooms, asparagus and onion at hand also.

Prepare a fire in a grill. Position the oiled grill rack 4–6 inches (10–15 cm) above the fire. Arrange the vegetables on the rack. Grill the fennel halves, artichoke halves, whole garlic heads and onion slices for about 12 minutes, the pepper halves and mushrooms for about 10 minutes, the endive halves for about 8 minutes, and the asparagus for 4–8 minutes, depending upon size. As the vegetables cook, turn them two or three times and brush with the oil mixture. Serve warm or at room temperature.

Serves 6

Herbed Two-Potato Skewers

3–4 boiling potatoes, about 1 lb (500 g)

2 small sweet potatoes or yams, about 1½ lb (750 g)

½ cup (4 fl oz/125 ml) olive oil

2 tablespoons chopped fresh parsley

1 tablespoon chopped fresh tarragon or thyme, or 1 teaspoon dried tarragon or thyme

¼ teaspoon red pepper flakes

½ teaspoon freshly ground pepper

½ teaspoon salt

Dark and crusty outside, soft and steamy inside. Good with grilled fish or chicken.

*P*repare a fire in a grill. Position the oiled grill rack 4 inches (10 cm) above the fire.

Steam all the potatoes on a rack over boiling water until they are barely tender when pierced, 15–20 minutes. Remove to a large bowl and cover with cold water. Let stand for about 2 minutes, then drain and pat dry with absorbent paper towels. Cut the potatoes into 1½-inch (4-cm) chunks and thread them onto skewers.

In a small bowl whisk together the oil, parsley, tarragon or thyme, red pepper flakes, pepper and salt; set aside. Arrange the skewers on the rack. Grill, turning frequently and brushing occasionally with the oil-herb mixture, until the potato skins are well browned, about 10 minutes.

Serves 6

Grilled Onion Slices

½ cup (4 oz/125 g) unsalted butter,
  melted
3 tablespoons Dijon mustard
2 teaspoons wine vinegar
1 tablespoon chopped fresh parsley or
  tarragon, optional
3 large red onions, cut crosswise into
  slices ½ inch (12 mm) thick
salt
freshly ground pepper

Grilled onions are quite sweet and not at all harsh. Although these go naturally with hamburgers, serve them with steaks and chops also, and even with meaty fish like swordfish. Green (spring) onions, which cook in just a few minutes, may be grilled with the same butter-mustard basting sauce.

Prepare a fire in a grill. Position the oiled grill rack 4–6 inches (10–15 cm) above the fire.

In a small bowl stir together the butter, mustard, vinegar, and the parsley or tarragon, if using.

Arrange the onion slices on the rack and sprinkle to taste with salt and pepper. Grill, turning two or three times and brushing with the butter-mustard mixture, until tender and golden, about 10 minutes.

Serves 6

Corn in the Husk

8 ears of corn, in the husk
4 tablespoons unsalted butter, at room
    temperature
salt
freshly ground pepper

*You're in for a treat if you haven't grilled corn before.
Do not worry if the husks burn and char; the kernels under-
neath stay moist. Serve with salt, pepper and plenty of
softened butter.*

*P*repare a fire in a grill. Position the grill rack 4–6 inches
(10–15 cm) above the fire.

Carefully peel back the husks on each ear of corn, but do
not detach. Remove and discard the silk. Rub each ear of
corn with ½ tablespoon butter and sprinkle to taste with salt
and pepper. Pull the husks back up around the corn and tie
them snugly at the top with heavy kitchen string. Arrange
the corn on the rack. Grill, turning frequently, until the
husks are blackened in spots, about 12 minutes.

Cut off the string, remove the husks and serve
immediately.

Serves 4

Grilled Eggplant and Fontina Sandwiches

1 large eggplant, about 3 inches (7.5 cm) in diameter and 6–7 inches (15–18 cm) long

salt for sprinkling on eggplant, plus ½ teaspoon

⅓ cup (3 fl oz/80 ml) olive oil

2 tablespoons fresh lemon juice

1 clove garlic, minced

1 tablespoon chopped fresh sage or 1 teaspoon dried sage

¼ teaspoon freshly ground pepper

5 oz (155 g) Fontina cheese, thinly sliced

handful of fresh sage leaves, optional

These have a good savory flavor and are delicious warm or at room temperature. They can even be reheated on the grill or in the oven the next day. If you can't find Fontina cheese, use Monterey Jack, mozzarella or any other mild cheese that will complement fresh sage.

Cover a baking sheet with absorbent paper towels. Cut the eggplant crosswise into slices about ½ inch (12 mm) thick. You should have 12 slices in all. Sprinkle both sides of each slice lightly with salt. Spread the slices out on the baking sheet and cover with more paper towels. Let stand for at least 1 hour, then rinse the slices and pat them dry.

In a jar with a tight-fitting lid, combine the oil, lemon juice, garlic, chopped or dried sage, ½ teaspoon salt and the pepper. Shake vigorously.

Prepare a fire in a grill. Position the oiled grill rack 4 inches (10 cm) above the fire. Arrange the eggplant slices on the rack. Grill, turning them once or twice and brushing with the oil mixture, until lightly browned, about 8 minutes. Top half of the slices with a piece of cheese and 2 or 3 sage leaves, if you have them, then cover with the remaining eggplant slices. Grill, turning once, until the cheese begins to melt, about 2 minutes longer.

Makes 6 sandwiches; serves 6

Glossary

The following glossary defines terms specifically as they relate to grilling. Included are major and unusual ingredients, essential equipment and basic techniques.

ANAHEIM CHILI
Slender chili pepper measuring 6–8 inches (15–20 cm) long, with a sharp, astringent, mild to medium-hot flavor. Sold fresh in its green state, sometimes labeled *chile verde,* or "green chili," New Mexico pepper or Rio Grande pepper. Also available roasted and canned as green chilies, as well as ripened until red and dried.

BABY BACK RIBS
Especially juicy and tender, small pork ribs cut from the top of a young animal's center loin section.

BARBECUE
Used generally to refer to grilling done outdoors over an open charcoal or wood fire, and to the equipment on which the food is grilled. More specifically, barbecue refers to long, slow **direct-heat cooking** on a spit or over an open pit above a cool fire, including liberal basting with a **barbecue sauce.**

BARBECUE SAUCE
Sweet, tart and spicy sauce used to **baste** foods or as a table condiment for grilled foods. Although recipes vary widely, common elements include tomato, sugar or molasses, vinegar, and a hot spice such as chili or mustard.

BASTE
To brush or otherwise coat food with the liquid in which it was marinated, a sauce, oil or butter, or some other liquid while it cooks, thereby keeping it moist and promoting a flavorful and attractive glaze on its surface. Basting should be performed at regular intervals during grilling.

BELGIAN ENDIVE (WITLOOF/CHICORY)
Leaf vegetable with refreshing, slightly bitter, spear-shaped leaves, white to pale yellow green in color and tightly packed in cylindrical heads 4–6 inches (10–15 cm) long.

BLANCH
To partially cook an ingredient, usually a vegetable, by immersing in boiling water for anywhere from a few seconds to a few minutes, depending upon the vegetable and the recipe. Certain vegetables should be blanched before grilling to ensure that they will cook through without burning.

BRAZIER
Simple grill with a shallow pan to hold the fire and a metal grid that, on some models, may be raised and lowered with a hand crank. Good for relatively quick grilling of individual servings, but not suited to roasts or whole poultry.

BRIQUETTES
Compact, uniformly shaped fuel made from compressed pulverized charcoal and an additive that facilitates lighting and burning. Provides good, spark-free heat, although less expensive brands may not burn as long or as hot as better-quality briquettes.

BRISKET
Large, flavorful cut of beef adjacent to the foreshank, composed of layers of meat and fat. Flat, oblong "first cut" brisket is leaner; triangular "front cut" has more flavor.

BROCHETTE
French term for **kabob,** food cooked on a **skewer,** derived from the word *broche,* meaning "pointed tool."

BUTTERFLYING
Horizontally cutting a large piece of meat, usually poultry or a leg of lamb, to open it out and flatten it into a shape roughly resembling a butterfly so that it cooks evenly on a grill (be careful not to cut it all the way through). Butterflying also usually involves boning the meat. Shrimp (prawns) may be butterflied too. While butterflying can be done at home, a quality butcher will do the job for you.

CARDAMOM
Sweet, exotic-tasting spice mainly used in Middle Eastern and Indian cooking. Its small, round seeds, which come enclosed inside a husklike pod, are best purchased whole, and the seeds ground as needed.

CAYENNE PEPPER
Very hot ground spice derived from dried cayenne chili pepper.

CHARCOAL, LUMP
Grilling fuel derived from a hardwood—such as mesquite, oak, hickory, alder, apple, pecan and cherry—that has been burned just until charred. Break the large chunks into smaller, more uniform pieces before lighting fire.

CHILI OIL
Popular seasoning of olive, sesame or vegetable oil in which hot chilies have been steeped. Available in gourmet markets, Asian food shops and the specialty-food aisle of the supermarket.

CHILI PEPPER
See specific varieties.

CHILI POWDER
Commercial blend of spices featuring ground dried chili peppers along with such other seasonings as cumin, oregano, cloves, coriander, pepper and salt. Best purchased in small quantities, because flavor diminishes rapidly after opening.

CHUTNEY
Refers to any number of spiced East Indian relishes or pickles served as condiments with meals and used as seasonings in cooking; most common are fruit-based chutneys. Available in ethnic markets and supermarket specialty-foods sections.

CILANTRO
Green, leafy herb resembling flat-leaf (Italian) parsley, with a sharp, aromatic, somewhat astringent flavor. Popular in Latin American and Asian cuisines. Also called fresh coriander and commonly referred to as Chinese parsley.

COMPOUND BUTTER
Blend of butter and herbs, spices or other seasonings, placed on top of grilled food at serving time to melt and form an instant sauce.

CORNISH GAME HEN
Small hybrid bird that usually yields a single serving. Although sometimes available fresh, they are most often found in the supermarket freezer section.

CURRY POWDER
Generic term for blends of spices commonly used to flavor East Indian–style dishes. Most curry powders will include coriander, cumin, **chili powder**, fenugreek and turmeric; other additions may include **cardamom**, cinnamon, cloves, allspice, **fennel** and **ginger**. Best purchased in small quantities, because flavor diminishes rapidly after opening.

DIJON MUSTARD
Mustard made in Dijon, France, from brown mustard seeds and white wine or wine vinegar. Pale in color, either smooth or coarse-grained, fairly hot and sharp-tasting, true Dijon mustard and non-French blends labeled Dijon style are widely available in supermarkets and gourmet stores.

DIRECT-HEAT COOKING
In grilling, refers to method of quickly cooking individual servings or relatively thin pieces of food by placing them on the grill rack directly above hot coals.

FENNEL
Crisp, refreshing bulb vegetable with a mild licorice flavor. Also known as anise and by its Italian name, *finocchio*. Other varieties are grown for their fine, feathery leaves, which are used as a fresh or dried herb, and for their small, crescent-shaped, dried seeds, which are used whole as a spice.

FLANK STEAK
Large, thin, fairly lean, boneless cut of beef.

GINGER
The root of the tropical ginger plant, which yields a sweet, strong-flavored spice. The whole root may be purchased fresh in the supermarket produce department. Dried and ground ginger is commonly available in jars or tins in the spice section.

GLAZE
To form a shiny, flavorful coating on food as it cooks, usually by **basting** it.

GRILLING
Outdoor or indoor cooking method in which food is placed on a metal grid directly over the heat source, whether charcoal, wood, gas or electric coil. The term also refers to cooking on a hot, flat metal surface.

GRILL RACK
Term for the metal grid upon which food to be grilled is placed.

HIBACHI
Small, inexpensive Japanese-style grill, usually square or rectangular in shape and often made of cast iron. Most hibachis are adequately sized to cook for two or three people.

HICKORY CHIPS
Small chips of the richly aromatic wood are usually soaked in water and then tossed onto glowing coals during cooking, to flavor the food with their smoke.

HOT RED PEPPER SAUCE
Bottled commercial cooking and table sauce made from fresh or dried hot red chilies. Many varieties are available, but Tabasco is the most commonly known brand.

INDIRECT-HEAT COOKING
In grilling, refers to method of cooking larger items that would burn if **direct-heat cooking** were employed. Glowing coals are pushed to perimeter of grill's fire pan, and food is placed in center of grill rack and usually covered to cook more slowly in the radiant heat.

JALAPEÑO CHILI
Extremely hot fresh chili pepper with a distinctively sharp flavor. A broad, tapering chili that measures about 1½ inches (4 cm) long and is usually dark green, although ripe red ones are occasionally available. When cutting or chopping, use kitchen gloves to protect hands from volatile chili oils if you have any cuts or abrasions; wash hands liberally with warm, soapy water after handling chilies, and avoid touching your eyes.

JUNIPER BERRIES
Aromatic, small dried berries of the juniper tree, used as a seasoning in marinades for meat or poultry.

KETTLE-TYPE GRILL
Grill with a deep fire pan and a high cover, both vented for temperature control, which enables long, slow, **indirect-heat cooking** of larger items. Its rounded bottom makes more efficient use of fuel.

MARINADE
Liquid, or sometimes dry, mixture of seasonings used to flavor and moisturize pieces of meat, poultry or seafood. The act of treating food with a marinade is known as marinating.

NEW YORK STEAK
Beef steak cut from the sirloin; prized for its tenderness and flavor.

KABOB
Middle Eastern and western term for **skewer** of bite-sized pieces of food cooked by grilling or broiling. Flat-bladed skewers help keep food pieces from twisting, ensuring more even cooking. Be sure to cut food into even-sized pieces.

To make kabobs from large pieces of seafood, meat or poultry (here, chicken breasts), first cut them into long, thin, fairly even strips.

The strips may be rolled into tight spirals and skewered or, as shown here, threaded back and forth on the skewer, either on their own or interspersed with chunks of vegetable.

OAK CHIPS
Small chips of the richly aromatic wood are usually soaked in water and then tossed onto glowing coals during cooking, to flavor the food with their smoke.

PAPRIKA
Powdered spice derived from the dried paprika pepper; popular in several European cuisines and available in sweet, mild and hot forms. Hungarian and Spanish paprikas are preferable.

PARAFFIN-SATURATED CORN COBS, BLOCKS OR STICKS
Easy-lighting fire starters, to be interspersed among charcoal.

POLENTA
Italian term for a cooked mush of specially ground cornmeal, which may be enriched with butter, cream, cheese or eggs. Served as a side dish. When cold, its consistency is firm enough for it to be shaped and grilled.

QUAIL
A small game bird—usually a single serving—with moist, tender, very flavorful meat.

RACK OF LAMB
Whole rib roast of very tender, uncut lamb chops. Most racks consist of seven ribs, although larger or smaller racks may be ordered from the butcher.

RED PEPPER FLAKES
Spice composed of coarsely ground flakes of dried red chilies, including seeds, which add moderately hot flavor to foods they season.

ROASTING
Cooking in the dry, radiant heat of an oven, a method well suited to large cuts of meat and whole poultry. Some types of grilling equipment—particularly **kettle-type grills**—may be used to roast with their lids closed, employing **indirect-heat cooking.**

ROSEMARY
Mediterranean herb, used either fresh or dried, with a strong aromatic flavor well suited to lamb and veal, as well as poultry, seafood and vegetables.

SAFFRON
Intensely aromatic, golden orange spice made from the dried stigmas of a species of crocus; used to perfume and color many classic Mediterranean and East Indian dishes. Sold either as threads—the dried stigmas—or in powdered form.

SAGE
Fresh or dried herb with a pungent flavor that goes especially well with fresh or cured pork, lamb and chicken.

SALSA
Latin American term for a cooked or fresh, raw sauce—most often one made with tomatoes, **tomatillos** or chilies.

SALT, COARSE OR KOSHER
Coarse-grained salt whose crystals are well suited for use in dry **marinades** for grilled foods.

SATÉ
Southeast Asian term for small **skewers** of spicy marinated meat, poultry or seafood. For most satés, the food is cut into long, thin ribbons through which the skewers are passed like a needle and thread through cloth.

SHALLOT
Small member of the onion family with brown skin, white-to-purple flesh, and a flavor resembling a cross between sweet onion and garlic.

SHIITAKE MUSHROOMS
Meaty-flavored Asian variety of mushrooms with flat, dark brown caps usually 2–3 inches (5–7.5 cm) in diameter. Available fresh in well-stocked greengrocers and fruit and vegetable departments; also sold dried, to be soaked in warm water to cover for approximately 20 minutes before use.

SKEWER
Thin metal or wooden stick upon which small pieces of meat, poultry, seafood or vegetables may be threaded for grilling. The pieces should not be threaded on the skewer too tightly.

SHRIMP
Peeling and Deveining
Fresh, raw shrimp (prawns) are usually sold with the heads already removed but the shells still intact. Before cooking on the grill, they should be peeled and their thin, veinlike intestinal tracts removed. After deveining, large shrimp are frequently **butterflied** to help them cook more evenly.

With your thumbs, split open the shrimp's thin shell along the concave side, between its two rows of legs. Peel away the shell, taking care to leave the last segment with tail fin intact and attached to the meat.

With a small, sharp knife, carefully make a shallow slit along the peeled shrimp's back, just deep enough to expose the long, usually dark-colored, veinlike intestinal tract. With the tip of the knife or your fingers, lift up and pull out the vein, discarding it.

To butterfly the shrimp, continue slitting down into the meat just far enough so that, with your fingertips, you can open it out and flatten it easily into two equal-sized lobes. Take care not to cut completely through the shrimp.

SKIRT STEAK
Thin, flavorful inexpensive cut of beef. May require special ordering from the butcher.

SMOKER
A grill with a lid sufficiently high to enclose a large piece of food. In the bottom is a fire pan for charcoal, gas or electric heat sources, upon which aromatic wood chips are placed to generate smoke. Above that may rest a pan to hold water, which rests below one or two layers of grill racks that hold the food being cooked beneath the domed cover. With water pan and lid removed, some smokers may be used as grills.

SMOKING
Process of cooking, curing or flavoring food with aromatic smoke. Hot smoking with intense, direct heat cooks food as it flavors it. Cold smoking, a longer process in which the food is subjected to smoke without heat, is used to cure foods such as salmon and ham. The addition of soaked wood chips or fresh or dried herbs to a grill fire during or toward the end of cooking also lends a smoky flavor to foods.

STARTER, CHIMNEY
Vertical, cylinder-shaped metal device very effective for quickly lighting **briquettes** or **charcoal.** Crumpled newspaper is placed under the metal grid near the bottom of the cylinder, the fuel is piled into the top, and then the paper is lit. Within about 20 minutes, coals are ready for cooking.

STARTER FLUID
Petroleum-based liquid poured over coals to facilitate lighting. Although once common, its use is now widely discouraged, since the fluid's fumes violate air-quality control standards in many areas.

Many alternative fire-starting methods exist, such as **paraffin-saturated corn cobs** and electric and chimney **starters.**

SOY SAUCE
Asian seasoning and condiment made from soybeans, wheat, salt and water. Seek out good-quality imported soy sauces; Chinese brands tend to be markedly saltier than Japanese.

SQUAB
Delicate-flavored, tender species of pigeon raised specifically for the table. The single-serving birds are available fresh or frozen from good-quality poulterers.

TANDOORI
East Indian style of cooking based on a charcoal-heated tandoor, a clay oven whose intense heat cooks food quickly, lightly charring its surface while keeping it tender and moist within. Tandoori-style marinades, which include yogurt and Indian spices, may be used to flavor foods to achieve a similar effect with any grill.

T-BONE STEAK
Tender, flavorful cut of beef from the center of the short loin, containing a small T-shaped bone.

TENDERLOIN
Tenderest portion of the short loin of beef, veal, lamb or pork.

TERIYAKI
Japanese style of grilling in which food is seasoned and basted with a **marinade** usually based on mirin—sweet rice wine—and **soy sauce,** to form a rich, shining **glaze.**

TOMATILLO
Small, green vegetable-fruit resembling—but not actually related to—the tomato. Fresh tomatillos, available in some Latin American markets and well-stocked supermarkets, usually come encased in brown papery husks, easily peeled off before tomatillos are cut. Canned tomatillos may be found in specialty-food sections of supermarkets.

TORTILLA
Thin, flat, round unleavened Mexican bread made from wheat flour or finely ground cornmeal; used as an edible wrapper for meat, poultry, seafood, cheese and other foods. Commercially manufactured tortillas are widely available in supermarkets and ethnic markets.

WORCESTERSHIRE SAUCE
Traditional English seasoning or condiment; an intensely flavorful, savory and aromatic blend of many ingredients, including molasses, **soy sauce,** garlic, onion and anchovies. Popular as a **marinade** ingredient or table sauce for grilled foods, especially red meats.

ZEST
Thin, brightly colored, outermost layer of a citrus fruit's peel, containing most of its aromatic essential oils; a lively source of flavor in **marinades** and seasoning mixtures. Zest may be removed with a simple tool known as a zester, drawn across the fruit's skin to remove the zest in thin strips; with a fine hand-held grater; or with a vegetable peeler or a paring knife. The latter tools are held almost parallel to the fruit's skin so that the zest may be cut off in thin strips and then thinly sliced or chopped on a cutting board.

TRUSSING
Binding a bird with heavy cotton or linen string to keep it compact during cooking, as well as to make it easier to lift from the grill. Linen string is best; it does not char easily. There are many ways to truss; this is one of the simplest:

Bend wing tips under body. Wrap and tie one length of heavy string (or two lengths of lighter string) around center of chicken, at thickest part of drumsticks, securing legs snugly to body. Bring tips of drum sticks together and tie securely with another length of string. Finally, with a third length of string, tie wings snugly to body.

Index

ACKNOWLEDGMENTS

The publishers would like to thank the following people and organizations for their generous assistance and support in producing this book:
Margaret D. Fallon, Janique Poncelet, Ruth Jacobson, Jane Fraser, Amy Morton, Ken DellaPenta, Rapid Lasergraphics (San Francisco), Danielle di Salvo, Maria Antonis, Stephen Griswold, Patrick Booth, the buyers for Gardener's Eden, and the buyers and store managers for Williams-Sonoma and Pottery Barn stores.

The following kindly lent props for the photography:
Sean Castelblanco, Stephanie Greenleigh, Sue Fisher King, Lorraine & Judson Puckett, Fredericksen Hardware, Sue White and Chuck Williams.